HOMEMADE MEMORIES

HOMEMADE MEMORIES

childhood treats with a twist

KATE DORAN

To Luke, home is wherever you are

CONTENTS

INTRODUCTION   6
    WHY HOMEMADE?   9
    INGREDIENTS   10
    EQUIPMENT   12
    SUPPLIERS   13

CRUMBS   15

STICKY FINGERS   45

CAKES   73

WHAT'S FOR PUDDING?   107

THE ICE CREAM VAN   145

MIDNIGHT FEASTS   179

DRINKS   207

LITTLE LOAF BASICS   231

INDEX   250

THANK YOU   255

INTRODUCTION

Close your eyes and think of your favourite childhood treat. Maybe it's a bowl of crumble, syrupy and steaming, a slab of chocolate cake, a chewy fruit pastille or a melting ice cream. Imagine how it looks and smells, the taste and texture, then let those senses transport you – to Sunday dinners with family and birthday parties with friends, giggly midnight feasts or days at the seaside, the air hot and sticky and the sand between your toes.

The way you're feeling right now? That's what I love about food.

Nicknamed 'the Little Loaf' aged three by a great aunt who noticed that my appetite for bread was bigger than I was, I fell in love with food from an early age. Not just eating – although that was a pretty big part – but everything that comes with it, from the preparation and cooking to the experience of sharing food with others and the way it can make you feel.

My mum was, and still is, a wonderful home cook, my dad an enthusiastic eater, and some of our fondest family memories can be measured in meals eaten and recipes made. Sugary treats were limited to special occasions – possibly one of the reasons I have such a sweet tooth now – but held in high regard and almost always homemade. Mum encouraged my brother and me to bake our own birthday cakes – a tradition I adore and uphold to this day – and together we'd spend happy hours in the kitchen, making a mess and eating the spoils.

In 2011 I started 'the Little Loaf' blog, a place to share my love of food and the stories that surround it. I taught myself how to make real, homemade bread – something we'd tried with Mum as children but never really mastered – and before long I was including sweet recipes as well. Baking my own bread made me think more about the benefits of making other food from scratch and I soon realised that I could not only recreate the classics I'd made in my childhood – crumbles and custards, cakes and ice cream – but homemade versions of shop-bought treats.

I started experimenting with familiar biscuit brands, all kinds of chocolates, sweets and – these are a game changer – homemade marshmallows: all things I'd never before considered could be made at home without industrial machines and unpronounceable ingredients. The process brought back all sorts of deliciously nostalgic memories which, when I shared them on the blog, seemed to resonate with readers. People from around the world started getting in touch, making my recipes and sharing stories of their own. It's then that the blog really began to feel like home.

Home in real life is a little flat in South West London where I live with my husband – and most enthusiastic recipe taster – Luke. I'm not a professional chef by trade – anything I didn't learn from my mum or granny I've taught myself through cookbooks, blogs and endless trial and error – but in a funny way I hope that this is reflected in my recipes. We're making homemade memories here, not packaged, professional ones: food for real people cooking in regular kitchens that can be perfectly delicious without being, well, perfect.

Cooking is a lot like telling stories. Ask two people to describe the same event and, despite the facts being exactly the same, their accounts will always be slightly different. So it is with a recipe: even if you follow the instructions to the letter, the results will be a fraction different each time. I've tried to make my recipes as foolproof as possible, but suggest you also embrace these little differences. The joy of making food at home rather than opening up a packet is that a bit of your personality goes into everything you make.

This book contains all of my childhood favourites, starting with biscuits and ending with a simple little loaf. In between there are doughnuts, jellies and crumbles, ice creams, sweets and enough sugar-dusted memories to savour long after the last crumb has been cleared away. My hope is that these recipes will last you a lifetime, that this book can be something you can curl up in bed with, turn to with a party to plan or when comfort is in need, cover with sticky fingerprints in the kitchen and use to create wonderful homemade memories all of your own.

Kate x

WHY HOMEMADE?

TASTE

There's nothing like licking the bowl to make you feel like a child in the kitchen again. Treats made from scratch almost always taste better too. Different from your shop-bought favourites, perhaps, but with real, recognisable flavours, which are ultimately the most delicious.

SMELL

However attached you are to a favourite brand of biscuit, it's hard to beat the smell of a freshly baked batch of ... well, pretty much anything emerging from the oven. Something to savour if you're on your own and guaranteed to entice the hungry hordes if you're catering for a crowd.

GOODNESS

There's enough flour, butter and sugar within these pages to make it clear this isn't a health book, but thinking about what you put in your body is important nonetheless. Homemade food might use ingredients high in fat or calories like butter, sugar and cream but (in moderation) they're still so much better for you than the chemicals, preservatives and other hidden ingredients you might not even know you're getting in shop-bought treats.

WASTE

Or lack of, to be precise. No environmentally-unfriendly packaging: just an airtight tin to house your homemade treats and the occasional napkin to clean up the crumbs when a finger won't do.

SATISFACTION

If, like me, you find pleasure in the process of making, sharing and eating delicious food, homemade is the only way to go. This is a book of recipes to make and share with your friends, family and loved ones, and I hope you'll find as much satisfaction in creating these treats as in eating them.

INGREDIENTS

Good ingredients are the first step towards great food, so use the very best that you can afford. Where substitutions are possible, I've made suggestions alongside individual recipes, otherwise please try to stick to the written ingredients and ratios for consistently delicious results.

ALCOHOL

If you're baking with children, teetotal or don't like the taste, I've suggested alternatives to alcohol unless it's intrinsic to a recipe. Most recipes only require a small quantity, so buy alcohol that you're also happy to drink.

BUTTER

Save your salty butter for spreading on bread and use unsalted as standard in these recipes.

To make brown butter (*beurre noisette*), melt the desired amount in a saucepan over a medium heat. Continue cooking – it will bubble and spit as the water content evaporates – for 2–3 minutes or until golden and nutty smelling. Transfer to a heatproof bowl to cool before using.

CHOCOLATE

I use dark chocolate with a cacao content above 60 per cent and milk chocolate above 30 per cent. White chocolate has no cocoa solids, but look for quality brands made from cocoa butter, sugar and milk solids only.

COCOA

All recipes use alkalised or Dutch-process unsweetened cocoa powder, the most commonly available in the UK. Green & Black's is a good brand and readily available.

COCONUT OIL

Unrefined coconut oil is the healthier option, but if you're not keen on the coconut flavour, look for odourless or refined. Biona is a great brand for both and available online.

DAIRY

Use full-fat milk, cream and yoghurt for the best results, organic if you can.

EGGS

All eggs in this book are large unless otherwise specified. Buy organic or free range, depending on what you can afford. When baking, use eggs at room temperature.

FLOUR

I use unbleached, stone-ground flour as standard, often adding nuttiness or texture with small amounts of wholemeal, wholemeal spelt or rye flour. If a recipe calls for self-raising flour and you don't have any to hand, combine 1 scant teaspoon of baking powder with every 100g flour required, whisking thoroughly before adding to the other ingredients.

FRUIT

Fruit can vary hugely in sweetness, so taste as you go and adjust accompanying sugar quantities accordingly. Always use unwaxed citrus fruit for zesting. If you can only find waxed, scrub under warm running water, rinse thoroughly, then pat dry before using.

LIQUID SWEETENERS

All honey in this book is runny. Look for dark maple syrup. Golden syrup can be substituted for honey at a pinch, but it won't taste quite the same. Malt extract is a syrupy substance available in specialist health-food shops or online. To measure honey and syrups easily, lightly grease your measuring spoon with vegetable oil first.

NUTS

Buy whole, raw nuts in small quantities and toast for individual recipes to ensure the freshest flavour.

SALT

I love using flaky Maldon sea salt in everything from cakes to ice cream and highly recommend that you do too. If a recipe calls for sifted ingredients, grind the flakes into a fine powder beforehand to ensure even dispersal.

SUGAR

I like to use golden caster and fudgy muscovado sugars, both light and dark, as standard. They have the best flavour.

VANILLA

I use either freshly scraped vanilla pods or extract. To make your own extract, see page 249.

EQUIPMENT

My kitchen is tiny so I appreciate that pace is an important factor when it comes to equipment, as well as the inevitable cost. I love the romantic notion of making everything with just my hands, a bowl and a wooden spoon, but in reality a few key pieces of equipment will make your life a whole lot easier in the kitchen.

BLENDER/FOOD PROCESSOR

Essential for grinding nuts, blitzing liquids, etc. I love my Magimix food processor, which can also be used to make pastry and cream ingredients for cakes instead of a stand mixer. Immersion or stick blenders are less powerful, but great if you're on a budget or tight on space.

ICE CREAM MACHINE

A great gadget if you're planning to make lots of ice cream. Try to find one with a minimum of 1 litre capacity. If you don't have an ice cream machine, don't worry: almost all the recipes in this book can be made without.

SCALES

If you're used to baking with cups or by eye, invest in an inexpensive digital scale and you'll never look back. An absolute must for accuracy.

MEASURING JUG AND SPOONS

When a recipe calls for water, milk or cream, I weigh them on my digital scales for accuracy: 1g = 1ml. For anything else, volume and weight is *not* the same thing so a measuring jug and spoons are essential.

MIXERS

I love using my KitchenAid stand mixer for everything from kneading bread and creaming butter to whipping up egg whites for meringue. When making marshmallows or nougat, a stand mixer is pretty essential. They are, however, expensive, so if the cost makes you feel faint, invest in a good quality hand-held electric mixer instead.

MOULDS

A handful of specialist moulds can turn everyday recipes into professional-looking showstoppers. My favourites are ice cream bar, ice-lolly and chocolate moulds, but all the recipes in this book offer an alternative if you don't have them.

OVEN

All the recipes in this book have been tested using a fan assisted or convection oven. I've provided temperatures for a conventional oven too, 20°C higher, but every oven varies slightly in temperature so get to know yours (you could buy an oven thermometer to check).

If you are baking biscuits or buns on two trays, you may need to swap them round half way through to ensure an even bake.

THERMOMETER

Just as a digital scale will revolutionise the accuracy of your recipes, so will a thermometer, especially when it comes to working with sugar for sweets. I use a Thermapen instant read digital thermometer, but less expensive alternatives are easily available.

TINS

I've tried to limit the number of tins used in this book to some key sizes:

- 500g and 1kg loaf tins
- 18cm, 20cm and 23cm square cake tins
- 20cm round cake tin
- 23cm fluted tart tin
- 12-hole muffin tin
- Swiss roll tin, approximately 20 x 30cm
- Deep-sided roasting tin, approximately 30 x 23cm
- Dariole moulds or ramekins approximately 175ml capacity

SUPPLIERS

Abbiamo.co.uk Stock the Silikomart range. I love their ice cream bar and chocolate moulds.

Brabantia.com/uk For inexpensive digital kitchen scales.

Cuisinart.co.uk Make good ice cream machines at a range of different prices.

Etsy Great for random vintage finds and pretty packaging. I found my ice cream cone rollers on Etsy but you can pick them up in most good kitchen shops.

KenwoodWorld.com/uk For hand-held electric mixers and stand mixers.

KitchenAid.co.uk Also great for stand mixers. I have one in candy apple red.

Lakeland.co.uk A handy one-stop shop for all sorts of cake tins, trays, biscuit cutters, gadgets and some ingredients.

LeCreuset.co.uk For tough-wearing saucepans and roasting dishes. Some chefs dismiss non-stick pans but I find them a lifesaver when it comes to sweet and caramel making.

Lekue.co.uk For silicone bakeware and a range of handy kitchen gadgets.

Magimix.uk.com For food processors. They're expensive but do the job and last forever.

SousChef.co.uk An Aladdin's cave of hard to find ingredients, kitchen equipment and more.

Squires-shop.com For modelling chocolate, cupcake cases and everything you could possibly want for decorating cakes.

CRUMBS

BISCUITS, COOKIES AND CRUMBLY THINGS

PEANUT BUTTER AND
JAMMIE DODGERS 18

WHOLEMEAL SPELT DIGESTIVES 21

OATY DUNKERS 22

MINI MARSHMALLOW TEACAKES 24

ALMOND, HONEY AND CINNAMON
FIG ROLLS 28

ORANGE, CARDAMOM AND
POPPY-SEED SHORTBREAD 30

JAFFA ORANGE CAKES 33

LEMON AND THYME CREAMS 34

REAL BOURBON BISCUITS 36

BROWN BUTTER
CHOCOLATE-CHUNK COOKIES 38

CARAMEL TEA AND BISCUIT SLICE 41

SPICED GINGERBREAD 42

When I was tiny, one of my favourite things to do when a friend came round was to make potions. Together we'd find the biggest bowl in the kitchen and fill it with ingredients like flour, toothpaste and food colouring to create a gloopy, inedible sludge.

It wasn't long before I realised my efforts might be better put towards making things I could actually eat, and one of my earliest kitchen memories is of learning to bake biscuits with my mum. We had a whole drawer full of different shaped cutters and together we'd roll out basic biscuit dough before stamping it into dinosaurs, elephants and their various edible friends.

After that, I learnt to make cakes, puddings and ice creams, but other kinds of biscuit mostly remained something that came from the shop. At school there were plastic packets of Hobnobs and Jammie Dodgers, Jaffa cakes at friends' houses and chocolate-filled Bourbons for special occasions. It wasn't until I had my own kitchen that I realised many of these shop-bought biscuits could be recreated at home.

Homemade biscuits and cookies are a happy revelation. There's something so satisfying about recreating your favourite branded treats from the comfort of your own kitchen and these biscuits also taste – hands down – so much more delicious than anything you can buy, baked with gorgeous, honest ingredients and a spoonful of love.

PEANUT BUTTER AND JAMMIE DODGERS

I wrote this recipe with peanut-butter-and-jam sandwich fans in mind, giving that all-American classic a biscuity twist. Freshly baked, these biscuits are crisp in contrast with their jammy middle; left a couple of days, they become softer and more sandwich-like. Either way, they're irresistible.

This is one recipe that works best made with shop-bought peanut butter, so save the home-made stuff (see page 238) for your toast and seek out a jar of smooth, natural peanut butter with no added sugar or salt to use here.

Makes about 30 dodgers

150g butter, softened
100g shop-bought smooth peanut butter
125g caster sugar
25g light muscovado sugar
1 egg yolk
1 tsp vanilla extract, homemade (see page 249) or shop-bought
large pinch salt
265g plain white flour, plus extra for dusting
about 100g of your favourite jam, homemade (see page 239) or shop-bought

In a medium bowl using a wooden spoon, or in a stand mixer fitted with the paddle attachment, cream together the butter and peanut butter for 1 minute. Add both sugars and beat for a further 2 minutes until fluffy. Add the egg yolk, vanilla and salt and beat until combined, then sift over the flour and mix to form a soft dough. Knead a couple of times until smooth.

Preheat the oven to 180°C/160°C fan/350°F/Gas mark 4. Line two baking trays with baking parchment.

On a lightly floured work surface, roll the dough to a thickness of 3–4mm. The dough will be quite fragile – if it breaks apart, gently press the crumbly edges back towards the centre, then carefully continue to roll.

Using a 5cm-biscuit cutter, cut out rounds of dough. Using a heart-shaped stamp, or another small cutter of your choice, cut a hole from the middle of half of the biscuits. Place all the biscuit rounds on the prepared baking trays.

Bake for 8–12 minutes until lightly golden. Keep a close eye on them – these biscuits can turn from golden to burnt very quickly. Remove from the oven, leave to cool on the trays for 5 minutes then transfer to a wire rack to cool completely.

When the biscuits are cool, spread a scant teaspoon of jam on the underside of the whole biscuits. Top each one with a cut-out heart biscuit and press down lightly.

The biscuits will keep in an airtight container for 2 days.

WHOLEMEAL SPELT DIGESTIVES

When I was at secondary school, one of my best friends lived just around the corner. Most evenings after school were spent at one another's houses pretending to do homework; her house being infinitely preferable for its endless supply of chocolate digestive biscuits.

Unlike industrial versions which use vegetable oil, these digestives are made with butter, resulting in a much more satisfying mouthful. Nowadays, I actually prefer my homemade digestives plain, but you could coat them with melted chocolate, if you like.

Blitz the oats to a fine powder in a food processor. Add the flour and butter and pulse until the mixture resembles fine breadcrumbs. If you don't have a food processor, use pre-ground oat flour and rub in the butter with your fingertips to achieve the same consistency.

Transfer to a medium bowl and add the wheatgerm, sugar, baking powder and salt, mixing with your hands to combine. Add the milk, a little at a time, bringing the mixture together to form a smooth, slightly sticky dough – you may not need all of the milk. Pat into a flattened disc, wrap in cling film and pop into the fridge to firm up for 15 minutes.

Preheat the oven to 180°C/160°C fan/350°F/Gas mark 4 and line two baking trays with baking parchment.

Remove the dough from the fridge, dust with flour and place between two sheets of cling film. Carefully roll to a thickness of about 3mm. Remove the cling film and cut out rounds using a 6cm biscuit cutter or the top of a glass tumbler, re-rolling any scraps. Carefully place on the prepared trays, a few centimetres apart.

Bake for 10–12 minutes, or until lightly golden. Leave to cool on the trays for 5 minutes then transfer to a wire rack to firm up and cool completely.

The biscuits will keep in an airtight container for 2–3 days.

Makes about 20 biscuits

65g rolled oats
100g wholemeal spelt flour, plus extra for dusting
100g cold butter, cubed
35g wheatgerm (or substitute with more ground oats)
55g light muscovado sugar
1 tsp baking powder
1 tsp salt
1–2 tbsp milk

Homemade hint

Try sandwiching two biscuits around toasted marshmallows (see page 204) and a couple of squares of your favourite chocolate for a British take on a s'more.

OATY DUNKERS

Described by a British comedian as the Royal Marines of the biscuit world due to their incomparable dunkability, Hobnobs are the perfect accompaniment to an afternoon cup of tea. Made with golden syrup then baked until crisp, my homemade version sits somewhere between a flapjack and the more conservative digestive. As with digestives, you can coat them in chocolate or leave them plain. Whichever you decide, one nibble is never enough.

Makes about 20 biscuits

125g butter, softened
80g light muscovado sugar
2 tbsp golden syrup
80g rolled oats
1 tbsp wheatgerm (or substitute with more rolled oats)
100g wholemeal or wholemeal spelt flour
½ tsp baking powder
½ tsp bicarbonate of soda
½ tsp salt

Preheat the oven to 180°C/160°C fan/350°F/Gas mark 4. Line two baking trays with baking parchment.

In a large bowl with a wooden spoon, or in a stand mixer fitted with the paddle attachment, cream together the butter and sugar for 2–3 minutes until pale and smooth. Add the golden syrup and beat to combine.

Stir in the oats and wheatgerm then sift over the flour, baking powder, bicarbonate of soda and salt. Tip any bran left in the sieve into the bowl and beat to form a sticky dough.

Take about two teaspoons of the dough and roll into a ball. Place on one of the prepared trays and press down lightly in the middle so that it spreads to about 4cm wide. Repeat with the remaining dough, leaving a few centimetres between each ball as they will flatten and expand as they bake.

Bake for 10–12 minutes until golden brown and the kitchen smells like toasty oats. Remove from the oven and leave to cool on the tray for a few minutes then transfer to a wire rack. Don't worry if the biscuits feel slightly soft; they should firm up and become crunchy as they cool.

The biscuits will keep in an airtight container for 3–4 days.

MINI MARSHMALLOW TEACAKES

——————————
• • • • • • • • •

When I first posted this recipe on my blog a few years back, I mentioned a tradition which both my husband and I independently grew up on of smashing a foil-wrapped teacake against your forehead to crack the chocolate before eating it. Some readers knew exactly what I was talking about; others thought I was completely mad.

Regardless of whether or not you uphold this tradition, these teacakes are deliciously messy both to make and to eat. And so much more fun because of it.

*Makes about
30 teacakes*

For the biscuit base
40g rolled oats
65g wholemeal or
wholemeal spelt flour,
plus extra for dusting
65g cold butter, cubed
1 tbsp wheatgerm (or
substitute with more
ground rolled oats)
30g light muscovado
sugar
¾ tsp baking powder
¾ tsp salt
1–2 tbsp milk

For the marshmallow
3 egg whites
150g caster sugar
2 tbsp golden syrup
pinch salt
½ tsp vanilla extract,
homemade (see page
249) or shop-bought

Blitz the oats to a fine powder in a food processor. Add the flour and butter and pulse until the mixture resembles fine breadcrumbs. If you don't have a food processor, use pre-ground oatmeal and rub in the butter with your fingertips to achieve the same consistency.

Transfer to a medium bowl and add the wheatgerm, sugar, baking powder and salt, mixing with your hands to combine. Add the milk, a little at a time, bringing the mixture together to form a smooth, slightly sticky dough. Pat into a flattened disc, wrap in cling film and pop in the fridge to firm up for 15 minutes. Don't leave it much longer or the dough will become too hard to roll.

Preheat the oven to 180°C/160°C fan/350°F/Gas mark 4 and line two baking trays with baking parchment.

Place the dough between two lightly floured pieces of cling film and roll to a thickness of 3–4mm. Use a 5cm round cutter or the top of a glass to cut out approximately 30 rounds of dough, re-rolling any scraps. Carefully transfer to the prepared baking trays, placing them a few centimetres apart, and bake for 10–12 minutes, or until lightly golden.

Remove from the oven and leave to cool completely on the trays.

To make the marshmallow filling, combine the egg whites, sugar, golden syrup and salt in a large heat-proof bowl set over a pan of barely simmering water. Make sure the bottom of the bowl doesn't touch the water or your eggs could scramble.

Whisk the mixture with a hand-held electric mixer on medium speed for 5–7 minutes until silky and roughly doubled in volume: it should be the texture of thickly whipped cream and hold firm peaks. Remove from the heat, add the vanilla and whisk on medium speed for a further 1–2 minutes until glossy and slightly cooled.

Transfer to a piping bag fitted with a plain 1cm nozzle and pipe a swirl on top of each biscuit. Leave to set at room temperature for 1 hour.

When ready to assemble, line a couple of trays with baking parchment and prepare the chocolate coating. Melt 300g of the chocolate in a heat-proof bowl over a pan of simmering water (make sure that the bowl doesn't touch the water). Remove from the heat and add the remaining chocolate and butter, or coconut oil, stirring until smooth. For a super-professional finish, follow the instructions for Tempered chocolate on page 188, omitting the butter/oil.

To coat, dip a teacake into the melted chocolate, spooning the chocolate over the top until completely covered. Using two forks – or your fingers – carefully remove the teacake from the chocolate, allowing any excess to drip back into the bowl. Place on one of the prepared trays then repeat with the remaining teacakes. Leave to set firm at room temperature for 1–2 hours.

The teacakes will keep in an airtight container for 2–3 days, in a cool place.

MINI PEANUT BUTTER TEACAKES

Spread each biscuit with a scant teaspoon of peanut butter (see page 238 or use shop-bought) before piping on the marshmallow.

For the chocolate coating
400g dark chocolate, chopped
50g butter or coconut oil (omit if using tempered chocolate)

ALMOND, HONEY AND CINNAMON FIG ROLLS

— · · · · · · · · · —

When my husband Luke was little, he was such a fig roll fan that his mum would always buy two packets at a time: one for the biscuit tin, and one which he would eat as soon as possible, by himself, in one sitting. I'm happy to say that this homemade version gets his seal of approval.

The tip for steaming the still-warm rolls in an airtight container after baking comes from pastry chef Stella Parks' Brave Tart blog and keeps them wonderfully soft. If you can bear to leave these biscuits for 24 hours before eating, the texture becomes even better.

Makes about 24 rolls

For the pastry
125g butter, softened
75g light muscovado
    sugar
1 egg yolk
seeds of ½ vanilla pod
75g plain white flour,
    plus extra for dusting
75g wholemeal flour
50g ground almonds
pinch ground cinnamon
pinch salt

For the filling
220g soft dried figs, any
    hard stalks removed
½ small eating apple,
    skin on, grated
1 heaped tbsp honey
1 tsp finely grated
    orange zest
2 tsp orange juice
pinch ground cinnamon
pinch salt

To make the pastry, cream together the butter and sugar in a large bowl or stand mixer fitted with the paddle attachment until pale. Beat in the egg yolk. Add the vanilla, flours, ground almonds, cinnamon and salt and gently mix to form a soft ball of dough. Flatten into a disc, wrap in cling film and chill for 15 minutes.

In a food processor, blitz the figs, apple, honey, orange zest and juice, cinnamon and salt to form a sticky paste.

Preheat the oven to 170°C/150°C fan/335°F/Gas mark 3. Line two baking trays with baking parchment. Remove the chilled dough from the fridge, place between two pieces of cling film and roll out to a large rectangle about 3mm thick. The dough will be quite fragile and sticky.

Cut the dough lengthways into three long strips. Spoon or pipe a third of the fig mixture down the centre of one strip and use a palette knife to help you gently fold one side on top, followed by the other, to create a long, enclosed tube. Press the edges of the pastry together to seal, then repeat with the remaining two strips. Use a sharp knife to cut each length of pastry into 5cm-wide rolls then place each one, seam side down, onto the prepared trays.

Bake for 20 minutes or until lightly golden and slightly puffed. Then carefully transfer to a plastic container with a lid to cool completely. This steaming gives them their characteristic cake-like texture.

The rolls will keep in an airtight container for 3–4 days.

ORANGE, CARDAMOM AND POPPY-SEED SHORTBREAD

While simple, three-ingredient shortbread is hard to beat, I love to build on the blank canvas of melting, buttery biscuit with layers of flavour and texture. These are fragrant with orange blossom water and cardamom and melt in the mouth. For a sandier texture, replace 40g of the flour with the same amount of semolina.

Makes 8 large pieces

200g butter, softened, plus extra for greasing
95g caster sugar, plus extra for sprinkling
2 tbsp poppy seeds
1 tsp orange blossom water
finely grated zest of 1 orange
200g plain white flour
85g cornflour
finely ground seeds from 8 cardamom pods or ¼ tsp ground cardamom
pinch salt

Preheat the oven to 170°C/150°C fan/335°F/Gas mark 3. Lightly grease a 23cm round loose-bottomed tart tin.

In a large bowl with a wooden spoon, a hand-held electric mixer or stand mixer fitted with the paddle attachment, cream the butter and sugar for 2–3 minutes until smooth, pale and fluffy. Add the poppy seeds, orange blossom water and orange zest and stir to combine.

Sift in the flour, cornflour, cardamom and salt gradually, mixing gently between each addition, until just incorporated (try not to over-mix).

Lightly and evenly press the dough into the prepared tin. Using a sharp knife, mark out lines for 8 large triangles, pressing about two thirds of the way into the dough with each slice of the knife. Prick each one with a fork.

Bake for 30–40 minutes or until golden blonde round the edges and no longer doughy in the middle. Remove from the oven, sprinkle with a little extra caster sugar and gently re-cut each triangle. Leave to cool completely in the tin.

The shortbread will keep in an airtight container for up to 1 week.

JAFFA ORANGE CAKES

Somehow greater than the sum of their parts, Jaffa cakes are one of my favourite teatime treats. And even though I'm thirty years old, I still like to lick off the chocolate then nibble carefully round the sponge until there's just a disc of wobbly orange jelly left. The sponge base is inspired by those irresistible French teacakes, financiers, but it's the zingy orange middle that really sets this recipe apart.

To make the jelly, combine the sugar and orange peel with 120ml water in a small saucepan. Bring to the boil then simmer for 10–15 minutes until the liquid has reduced by about half.

Meanwhile, line an 18cm square tin with cling film. Place the gelatine sheets in a bowl of cold water and soak for 5 minutes.

Remove the syrup from the heat and strain into a measuring jug. Squeeze as much water as possible out of the gelatine leaves, then stir them into the warm syrup until dissolved. Stir in the orange juice before straining into the lined tin. Chill for 2 hours, or until firm.

To make the cakes, measure out 30ml of the browned butter and set aside. Use the remaining brown butter to grease a 12-hole muffin tin. Preheat the oven to 190°C/170°C fan/375°F/Gas mark 5.

Sift the icing sugar and flour into a bowl, then whisk in the ground almonds and orange zest. Add the egg whites, salt and the cooled brown butter and whisk to a thick batter.

Divide the batter between the muffin tin holes and bake for 9–12 minutes until the cakes are lightly golden and firm to the touch. Remove from the oven and leave to cool in the tin completely.

When the jelly has set, use a 4cm cutter to cut out discs from the layer of jelly. Carefully place one disc on top of each cooled cake.

To finish the cakes, melt the chocolate in a heat-proof bowl suspended over a pan of barely simmering water (or in the microwave) and leave to cool for 10–15 minutes. Carefully spoon 1–2 teaspoons of melted chocolate over the top of each jelly disc, coating the top of each cake. Leave to cool completely.

The cakes will keep in an airtight container for 2 days.

Makes 12 cakes

For the orange jelly
60g caster sugar
peel from 1 large orange
3 sheets platinum-grade fine leaf gelatine
100ml orange juice (from about 2 large oranges)

For the cakes
40g browned butter (see page 10), cooled
60g icing sugar
20g plain white flour
40g ground almonds
¼ tsp finely grated orange zest
2 egg whites, lightly beaten
pinch salt

To finish
120g dark chocolate, chopped

LEMON AND THYME CREAMS

This is my less-than-traditional take on a classic custard cream. Herbs and citrus might sound more like something you'd put inside a Sunday roast than a sweet biscuit, but trust me on this one: the combination really works.

When baking, these biscuits have an aromatic, almost savoury smell, but the end result has just the right balance of sweetness and perfume. This recipe also works well made with lavender or rosemary in place of the thyme.

Makes about 15 sandwich biscuits

For the biscuits
140g plain white flour,
   plus extra for dusting
50g icing sugar
pinch salt
100g cold butter, cubed
finely grated zest of
   1 lemon
2 tsp fresh thyme
   leaves, finely chopped
1 egg yolk

For the lemon buttercream
75g butter, softened
175g icing sugar, sifted
finely grated zest of
   1 lemon
1 tbsp lemon juice

Preheat the oven to 170°C/150°C fan/335°F/Gas mark 3. Line two baking trays with baking parchment.

Sift together the flour, icing sugar and salt into a large bowl. Using your fingertips, lightly rub in the butter until the mixture resembles breadcrumbs. Add the lemon zest, thyme and egg yolk and mix until a ball of dough forms, being careful not to overwork the dough or it will become tough.

Transfer the dough to a lightly floured work surface and roll it out to a thickness of 4–5mm. Use a 6cm fluted biscuit cutter to cut out circles – you should have enough dough to make about 30 biscuits. Carefully transfer the biscuits to the prepared baking trays and bake for 10–12 minutes until lightly golden at the edges. Remove from the oven and leave to cool on the trays for 5 minutes then transfer to a wire rack to cool completely.

To make the buttercream, beat the butter for 1 minute. Add the icing sugar, lemon zest and juice and cream together until light and fluffy, starting slowly so that the icing sugar doesn't billow up. If the mixture seems too dry, add more lemon juice, a few drops at a time.

Sandwich the cooled biscuits together with the buttercream, pressing them together gently to avoid breaking. If you prefer a neater finish, use a piping bag.

The filled biscuits will keep in an airtight container for 2–3 days.

REAL BOURBON BISCUITS

Bourbon biscuits may bear absolutely no relation to the alcohol of the same name, but they are infinitely improved by it. I first made this recipe as a gimmick for my husband to take away with him on a boozy boys weekend, but the flavours worked so well that a couple of tweaks later it became my go-to chocolate sandwich biscuit.

The bourbon gives a subtle lift to these deeply chocolaty biscuits, but if you're teetotal or serving them to children, replace the alcohol with the same quantity of orange juice or milk.

Makes 20–24 biscuits

For the biscuits
100g butter, softened
75g light muscovado
    sugar
25g caster sugar
2 tbsp golden syrup
220g plain white flour
50g cocoa powder
1 tsp bicarbonate of
    soda
pinch salt
3 tbsp milk

For the buttercream filling
100g butter, softened
175g icing sugar
2 tbsp cocoa powder
3–4 tsp bourbon (to
    taste)
½ tsp vanilla extract,
    homemade (see page
    249) or shop-bought

Preheat the oven to 170°C/150°C fan/335°F/Gas mark 3. Line two baking trays with baking parchment.

In a medium bowl with a wooden spoon, or in a stand mixer fitted with the paddle attachment, cream together the butter and both sugars for 2–3 minutes until pale and fluffy. Beat in the golden syrup, then sift in the flour, cocoa, bicarbonate of soda and salt and beat together to combine. Add the milk, a little at a time, to make a smooth dough.

Place the dough between two large pieces of cling film – this will stop it sticking to the work surface without needing to use flour, which can mark the biscuits. Roll out to a large rectangle 3–4mm thick. Cut into rectangles 6 x 3cm, re-rolling any scraps, then transfer to the prepared baking trays and use a wooden skewer to mark out rows of dots along the length of each biscuit.

Bake for 10 minutes then remove from the oven. Leave to cool on the tray for 5 minutes then transfer to a wire rack to cool completely.

To make the filling, cream the butter for 2 minutes until fluffy. Sift in the icing sugar and cocoa and beat slowly (and carefully as the icing sugar will billow up) until combined. Add the bourbon and vanilla extract and beat until smooth.

Spoon or pipe a thick line of buttercream down the middle of one biscuit. Sandwich together with a second biscuit and repeat until all the biscuits are filled.

The filled biscuits will keep in an airtight container for 3–4 days.

BROWN BUTTER CHOCOLATE-CHUNK COOKIES

I can clearly remember the first chocolate chip cookie I ever ate. My brother had been baking at a Canadian friend's house and brought home a freshly made batch. Still warm and soft, yet crisp round the edges, they were different from any British biscuit I'd ever eaten. It was love at first bite.

Made with chocolaty chunks and nutty brown butter, these cookies are my unashamedly extravagant interpretation of that recipe. The dough benefits from a 24-hour rest in the fridge, so start this recipe the day before you want to bake the cookies.

Makes about 15 cookies

115g butter
100g plain white flour
100g wholemeal flour
½ tsp baking powder
½ tsp bicarbonate of soda
pinch salt
110g soft light brown sugar
60g caster sugar
1 egg, lightly beaten
2 tsp vanilla extract, homemade (see page 249) or shop-bought
100g dark chocolate, roughly chopped
75g milk chocolate, roughly chopped

Homemade hint

Double the recipe and freeze half the dough to always have emergency cookies on hand. To bake from frozen, add 1–2 minutes to the baking time.

Line two baking trays that will fit in your fridge with baking parchment. In a medium saucepan, brown the butter (see page 10) then set aside to cool for 10 minutes.

In a medium bowl, whisk together the flours, baking powder, soda and salt.

In a stand mixer fitted with the paddle attachment, or in a medium bowl with a hand-held electric mixer, beat together the cooled brown butter and both sugars. A slightly gritty texture is fine. Add the egg and vanilla and beat until just combined.

Gently fold in the flour mixture, followed by all the chopped chocolate.

Using your hands, scoop out about 40g of dough and roll into a ball. Place onto one of the prepared trays and flatten slightly. Repeat with the remaining dough, leaving a generous 5cm or so between each one. Cover with cling film and chill overnight, or for a minimum of 8 hours.

When ready to bake, preheat the oven to 190°C/170°C fan/375°F/Gas mark 5. Remove the cookie trays from the fridge and bake for 8–12 minutes until golden and set round the edges but still slightly soft in the middle. The cookies will firm up as they cool so err on the side of under-baked.

Allow to cool on the trays for 3–4 minutes. The cookies will keep in an airtight container for up to 5 days.

CARAMEL TEA AND BISCUIT SLICE

———————————————
· · · · · · · ·

Tea and biscuits were made for each other, so what better than a recipe that combines the two? Here, caramel infused with tea leaves adds a depth of flavour and counterpoint to the sweetness of classic millionaire's shortbread. These are incredibly rich, so serve in thin slices.

Preheat the oven to 170°C/150°C fan/335°F/Gas mark 3. Lightly grease a 20cm square baking tin.

In a large bowl cream together the butter and sugar until smooth and pale. Sift over the flour, cornflour and salt then add the lemon zest, mixing gently until combined.

Lightly press the dough into the prepared tin and bake for 30–40 minutes or until pale golden round the edges. Remove from the oven and leave to cool completely.

Bring the milk to a gentle simmer. Add the tea leaves, stir, then remove from the heat and leave to infuse for 5 minutes. Strain the infused milk into a large saucepan then add the sugar, golden syrup, vanilla seeds and pod, bicarbonate of soda and salt. Bring to the boil, stirring occasionally to prevent sticking. Reduce the heat slightly and continue to cook, stirring frequently, until the mixture begins to thicken.

Reduce the heat to a low simmer. Continue to cook, stirring continuously, until it has the consistency of thick caramel sauce. Take the pan off the heat, remove the vanilla pod and pour over the shortbread in an even layer. Chill for 1 hour, or until firm.

In a heat-proof bowl suspended over a pan of simmering water (make sure that the bowl doesn't touch the water), or in the microwave, melt the milk chocolate and butter. Pour the melted chocolate over the caramel and spread out evenly. Melt the white chocolate in a separate bowl and drizzle over the top, using a toothpick to swirl the chocolates, creating a marbled effect. Chill for 1 hour, or until firm.

Carefully remove the shortbread from the tin and cut into slices.

The slices will keep in an airtight container for up to 1 week.

Makes about 14 slices

For the shortbread
200g butter, softened, plus extra for greasing
95g caster sugar, plus extra for sprinkling
200g plain white flour
85g cornflour
pinch salt
1 tsp finely grated lemon zest

For the milk caramel
(or substitute 300ml shop-bought dulce de leche)
1 litre milk
1 tbsp Earl Grey tea leaves, or tea leaves of your choice
225g caster sugar
1 heaped tbsp golden syrup
seeds of half a vanilla pod
¼ tsp bicarbonate of soda
large pinch salt

For the topping
180g milk chocolate, broken into pieces
25g butter, cubed
40g white chocolate, broken into pieces

SPICED GINGERBREAD

Eating gingerbread men always demands a certain sense of ceremony. I can never decide whether to devour the head first in cannibalistic glee or slowly nibble my way around their various gingery limbs. I like my gingerbread packed with plenty of spice, the zing of orange zest and a double hit of ginger. Make these as men, women, animals or any shape your heart desires: the quantity of biscuits you'll end up with will vary accordingly.

Makes about 16 gingerbread men or 24 biscuits

350g plain white flour, plus extra for dusting
1 tbsp ground ginger
1 tsp ground cinnamon
½ tsp ground allspice
pinch ground cloves
pinch freshly ground black pepper
1 tsp bicarbonate of soda
pinch salt
100g cold butter, cubed
145g light brown muscovado sugar
1 egg
3 tbsp golden syrup
1 tbsp black treacle
2 tsp freshly grated ginger
finely grated zest of half a small orange

Preheat the oven to 180°C/160°C fan/350°F/Gas mark 4. Line two baking trays with baking parchment.

Sift the flour, ground spices, bicarbonate of soda and salt into a medium bowl. Quickly rub in the butter with your fingertips until the mixture resembles fine breadcrumbs (you can also do this in a food processor). Mix in the sugar.

In a small bowl, whisk together the egg, golden syrup, treacle, fresh ginger and orange zest. Pour into the flour mixture and mix to form a soft, smooth dough.

Transfer the dough to a lightly floured work surface and immediately roll out to a thickness of about 3–4mm – slightly thicker if you prefer a softer biscuit, slightly thinner to make them really crisp. Cut out gingerbread men or any other shapes you like, re-rolling any scraps to make as many biscuits as possible. Carefully transfer to the prepared trays.

Bake for 10 minutes or until golden and the smell of ginger fills the room. Remove from the oven, allow to cool for a few minutes on the trays then transfer to a wire rack to cool completely. The biscuits will crisp up as they cool.

The gingerbread will keep in an airtight container for 2–3 days.

STICKY FINGERS

HAND-HELD TREATS FOR ANY TIME OF DAY

BLACKBERRY AND HAZELNUT
MERINGUE SANDWICHES   48

OAT AND RAISIN BUTTERMILK SCONES   50

FIG AND RYE ROCK BUNS   52

APRICOT, PEANUT AND SESAME FLAPJACKS   54

PECAN CARAMEL APPLES   56

SALTY-SWEET POPCORN   59

ORANGE AND HONEY ICED BUNS   60

JAM-PACKED DOUGHNUTS   61

BANOFFEE PECAN ÉCLAIRS   64

MALT WHISKY LOAF   68

WHOLEMEAL TOASTER PASTRIES   70

When I was growing up, sweet treats were fairly limited in 'the Little Loaf' household. One Halloween a group of trick or treaters arrived at our door, head to toe in spooky costumes and hands held out for whatever sweets Mum had to offer. After a few minutes rummaging round the cupboards, she returned with a fun-sized packet of raisins to share amongst the group.

This story is one we love to tease my mum with, but for every one like it I've got a sugar-coated memory to sit alongside. On Saturday mornings my brother and I were allowed to visit the local bakery while my parents were still in bed, eyeing up rows of elegant éclairs and jam-packed doughnuts. On Bonfire night we'd eat toffee apples until our teeth stuck together. And every time we went to visit my granny, she'd emerge from the larder with a squidgy malt loaf, chubby iced fingers or bumpy rock buns.

Food tastes amazing when you eat it with your hands. I'm talking fingers and chins sticky with jam from doughnuts, scones piled high with clotted cream and flaky pastries that burst their contents with every bite. These are treats for eating with your hands at any time of day, so embrace the mess and enjoy this chapter in all its sugar-dusted glory.

BLACKBERRY AND HAZELNUT MERINGUE SANDWICHES

Swirled through with cocoa and cinnamon then sandwiched round a filling of blackberry whipped cream, these delicate meringues are a world away from the pre-made nests found in the shops. Chill for an hour before serving and the meringue will soften slightly into the cream, making them easier to eat. These are also delicious served with Hot chocolate fudge sauce (see page 247).

Makes 8–10 sandwiches

For the meringue
30g hazelnuts, skin on
2 egg whites, at room temperature
pinch salt
135g caster sugar
1 scant tbsp cocoa powder
1 tsp ground cinnamon

For the filling
150g blackberries
2 tsp apple juice or water
175ml double cream
seeds of half a vanilla pod

Preheat the oven to 180°C/160°C fan/350°F/Gas mark 4. Spread the hazelnuts on a tray and roast for 8–10 minutes. Remove from the oven, allow to cool, then rub off the papery skins with a tea towel. Roughly chop or blitz in a food processor and set aside.

Reduce the oven temperature to 120°C/100°C fan/250°F/Gas mark ½ and line two baking trays with baking parchment.

In a large, clean, dry bowl, whisk the egg whites and salt until soft peaks form. Add 120g of the caster sugar, a tablespoon at a time, whisking well after each addition. Continue whisking until really thick and glossy.

Sift over the cocoa powder and cinnamon. Gently fold into the meringue mixture using a large metal spoon. Spoon or pipe discs approximately 5cm wide onto the prepared baking trays, a few centimetres apart. Bake for 1½–2 hours until crisp. Turn off the oven and leave them inside to cool completely.

To make the filling, combine the blackberries and apple juice in a small saucepan. Cook over a gentle heat until the fruit softens and releases its juices. Press through a fine mesh sieve, collecting the blackberry purée in a small bowl and allow to cool completely.

Whip the cream with the remaining caster sugar until soft peaks form. Fold in the vanilla seeds and blackberry purée. Sandwich together the meringues with the cream filling, rolling the edge of each 'sandwich' in the chopped nuts. Chill for 30 minutes–1 hour before serving (any longer and they may start to soften too much). Eat immediately.

The unfilled meringues will keep in an airtight container for up to 2 weeks.

OAT AND RAISIN
BUTTERMILK SCONES

· · · · · · · ·

The best scones are always light, but I like mine with a little texture too. Here buttermilk makes for a soft, tender crumb, studded with juicy tea-plumped fruit and sprinkled with oats.

Wholesome yet delicate, these scones are delicious split open and served warm with your favourite jam and thick clotted cream. Remember to soak the raisins for at least one hour before you begin.

In a small bowl, combine the raisins or sultanas and warm tea. Leave to soak for 1–2 hours.

Preheat the oven to 220°C/200°C fan/425°F/Gas mark 7. Line 2 baking trays with baking parchment.

In a large bowl, sift together the flours, icing sugar, baking powder and salt. Tip any bran left in the sieve into that bowl. Add the butter and gently rub with your fingertips until the mixture resembles fine breadcrumbs. A few streaks of butter are absolutely fine. Drain the raisins or sultanas (discarding any tea that hasn't been soaked up) and mix into the dry ingredients.

Make a well in the middle of the mixture and pour in the buttermilk. Use a table knife to stir the mixture until it comes together to a soft, even dough. If it feels too dry, add a little more buttermilk, a teaspoon at a time.

Lightly dust the work surface with flour and turn out the dough. Knead once or twice to get rid of any cracks then gently pat into a round 2–3cm thick. You don't want to roll this dough or you'll knock out too much air and the scones won't rise so well.

Dust a 6cm fluted cutter with flour and cut out rounds as close to each other as possible. Re-roll any scraps, but bear in mind that the scones made from these won't be quite as light.

Place the scones on your prepared baking trays and brush the tops with beaten egg. Mix together the oats and demerara sugar, sprinkle over the top of the scones then bake for 12–14 minutes until risen and golden. Remove from the oven and allow to cool slightly before serving with plenty of jam and cream.

The scones are best eaten warm on the day of making, but will keep in an airtight container for 2 days. Reheat at 170°C/150°C fan/335°F/Gas mark 4 for a few minutes, if you like.

Makes about
15 scones

125g raisins or sultanas
80ml strongly brewed
    black tea, warm
300g plain white flour,
    plus extra for dusting
50g wholemeal flour
2 tbsp icing sugar
3 tsp baking powder
pinch salt
75g cold butter, cubed
215ml buttermilk or
    natural yoghurt,
    thinned with a little
    water
1 egg yolk, lightly
    beaten, to glaze
25g rolled oats
1 tbsp demerara sugar

FIG AND RYE ROCK BUNS

Until I started making my own, I don't think I'd eaten a rock bun anywhere other than at my granny's house. Just one taste and I'm transported straight back to her kitchen table; afternoons spent playing cards, eating cake and sneaking any scraps to her two black Labradors when I thought no one was looking.

Rock buns won't win any beauty contests, but for me that only adds to their appeal. Served warm, spread thick with salty butter, these rustic little buns are best eaten within a few hours of making: the antithesis of packaged food and a reminder that life is for living in the moment.

Makes about 15 buns

125g rye flour
100g plain white flour
65g caster sugar
2 tsp baking powder
½ tsp ground cinnamon
125g cold butter, cubed
175g soft dried figs, any
    hard stems removed
    and roughly chopped
80–100ml milk
1 egg
finely grated zest of half
    an orange plus extra
    for sprinkling
demerara sugar, for
    sprinkling

Preheat the oven to 190°C/170°C fan/375°F/Gas mark 5. Line two baking trays with baking parchment.

Put the flours, sugar, baking powder and cinnamon in a bowl. Add the butter and rub together with your fingertips until the mixture resembles soft, fine breadcrumbs. Stir in the chopped figs.

In a jug or small bowl, beat 80ml of the milk with the egg and orange zest. Pour into the dry ingredients then carefully mix to a sticky dough. The dough should be stiff but spoonable: add a little more milk if necessary. Take care not to over-work it or the dough can become tough.

Scoop heaped tablespoons of the mixture onto your prepared baking trays, leaving a few centimetres between each one. You want them to look rounded but slightly craggy. Sprinkle each bun with a little demerara sugar and bake for 20–25 minutes until firm and golden.

Remove the buns from the oven. Use a palette knife to loosen them from the parchment, leave them to cool slightly on the trays then transfer them to a wire rack. Sprinkle with a little more orange zest, if you like.

The rock buns are best eaten on the day of making.

APRICOT, PEANUT AND SESAME FLAPJACKS

My mum has always enjoyed sneaking good-for-you ingredients into otherwise indulgent meals. Replacing some of the butter and golden syrup in flapjacks with peanut butter and honey might not be the most virtuous of her substitutions, but it's delicious and one that I replicate to this day.

Apricots and sesame seeds give these flapjacks a toffee-like texture and toasty taste. I like mine crisp on the outside and slightly squidgy in the middle: for a more biscuity treat, turn the oven temperature up by 10°C and bake for a few minutes more.

Makes 16

100g butter, plus extra
    for greasing
100g smooth or crunchy
    peanut butter,
    homemade (see page
    238) or shop-bought
100g light muscovado
    sugar
4 tbsp honey
150g dried apricots,
    roughly chopped
135g rolled oats
90g jumbo rolled oats
3 tbsp sesame seeds
finely grated zest of
    1 small orange

Preheat the oven to 180°C/160°C fan/350°F/Gas mark 4. Grease and line a 20cm square baking tin with baking parchment.

In a medium saucepan, gently heat the butter, peanut butter, sugar and honey, stirring to combine. Add the apricots and cook for 1–2 minutes to soften them slightly, then remove from the heat and stir in both oats, the sesame seeds and orange zest.

Scrape the mixture into your prepared tin, pressing down firmly and evenly with the back of a spoon or spatula. Bake for 25–30 minutes until golden brown round the edges and set in the middle.

Remove from the oven and leave to cool completely in the tin. The flapjacks will firm up as they cool so don't attempt to cut them while still warm.

Once cool, remove from the tin and use a sharp knife to slice into squares.

The flapjacks will keep in an airtight container for up to 1 week.

PECAN CARAMEL APPLES

The classic accompaniment to bonfires and fireworks, toffee apples always look so inviting in their shiny cellophane wrappers. As a child I loved nibbling at the crunchy sugar coating but would usually stop short at the apple itself, often powdery and disappointing.

There's no room for disappointment here with crisp, juicy apples inside a soft caramel coating. If you buy British, your apples are unlikely to be waxed; if for any reason they are, wash the wax off thoroughly with warm water or the caramel coating won't stick.

Makes 6–8 caramel apples

6–8 medium apples (crisp and British, if possible)
1 x batch Rosemary sea salt caramels (see page 192) or shop-bought chewy caramels
2 tbsp double cream
150g pecan halves, roughly chopped

Remove the stalks from the apples and insert a wooden lolly stick in the top of each one. Chill for 1 hour.

Line a tray that will fit in your fridge with baking parchment.

In a large, heavy-bottomed saucepan, combine the caramels and cream over a low heat, stirring until melted. Allow to cool for 1–2 minutes.

Dip the apples in the caramel one at a time, spooning the caramel over the top until the apples are completely coated. Let any excess caramel drip back into the saucepan, then roll the underside of each apple in the chopped nuts. Place on the prepared tray and chill until completely firm (about 15 minutes).

These caramel apples are best eaten on the day of making.

PECAN CARAMEL PEARS

Caramel pears are a lovely alternative to apples. Choose fruit that is still a little bit firm to ensure that it stays on the stick.

SALTY-SWEET POPCORN

I can't tell you the number of times I've smuggled food into the cinema. My husband readily admits to hiding sweets up his sleeves as a child and my friends and I used to sneak all sorts in underneath our jumpers including, of course, popcorn.

Homemade popcorn is fun to make, inexpensive and so much more delicious than anything you can buy, regardless of whether you eat it at home on the sofa or sneak it into the cinema.

Makes one large bowlful

2 tbsp groundnut or coconut oil
150g popcorn maize kernels
75g butter
3 tbsp caster sugar
generous pinch salt

In a large saucepan, combine the oil and a pinch of kernels (about 5). Cover with a lid and warm over a medium-high heat. When the kernels pop, add the remaining corn, cover with a lid and shake once or twice to coat in the oil.

Cook for 2–3 minutes, shaking the pot every 30 seconds or so to prevent sticking or burning. A few kernels will pop at first, then the rest will follow in a noisy flurry. After about 1 minute, remove from the heat and shake again: the residual heat should pop the last remaining kernels. You'll know the popcorn is done when you no longer hear popping.

Pour the popped corn into a large bowl. Return the pan to a low heat, discarding any un-popped kernels, and add the butter. Allow to melt, then when the butter begins to brown pour it over the popcorn. Sprinkle over the sugar and salt, then toss with your hands until evenly coated. Taste, adding a little more sugar and salt if necessary, then toss again.

The popcorn is best eaten on the day of making, straight out of the bowl (or smuggled into the cinema).

ORANGE AND HONEY
ICED BUNS

Iced buns always make me think of sports. It might sound an unlikely combination, but whenever we played another team at netball in primary school, half-time was marked by a tray of iced fingers and segments of fresh orange.

Sweet iced bun and orange make for a tasty match, so here I've combined the two. This is the same dough as used in my doughnuts, with some orange zest added. For a fancier treat, split the buns open once the icing has set and fill with homemade Strawberry, plum and vanilla jam and Whipped cream (see pages 239 and 248).

Makes a baker's dozen

For the buns
**1 x quantity doughnut
   dough (see opposite)**

For the icing
**1 tsp finely grated
   orange zest
2 tbsp orange juice
1 tbsp honey
250g icing sugar**

Homemade hint

This recipe makes a baker's dozen, i.e. 13 buns, as I like to have one ball of dough to practise shaping on without messing up the main batch.

Line a large baking tray with baking parchment. Follow the instructions to make the dough up to the first rise (see opposite) then scrape the dough out of the bowl onto a lightly floured work surface. Divide into 13 equal sized pieces – about 60g each. Roll each piece into a ball then stretch out to a finger shape about 12cm long.

Place the fingers of dough on the prepared baking tray, leaving a couple of centimetres gap between each one. Cover with a tea towel and leave to rise for a further hour or until doubled in size and just touching each other.

Preheat the oven to 200°C/180°C fan/400°F/Gas mark 6.

Once risen, remove the tea towel and bake for 8–10 minutes until pale golden. Remove from the oven, transfer the buns to a wire rack and leave to cool completely.

To make the icing, warm the orange zest and juice along with the honey in a heat-proof bowl suspended over a pan of simmering water, stirring to combine. Remove from the heat, sift over the icing sugar and whisk until smooth.

Separate the buns and, one at a time, dip the top half in the icing, swiping your finger flat along the surface to smooth. Leave the icing to firm up at room temperature.

The iced buns will keep in an airtight container for 2 days.

JAM-PACKED DOUGHNUTS

— — — — • • • • • • • • • •

Lip-smacking, deep-fried, sugary goodness with just the right amount of grease, these are inspired by the doughnuts my mum would allow us on special occasions. Making your own is immensely satisfying, especially when eaten plump with homemade jam and still warm from the pan.

You don't need a deep-fat fryer here, just a deep-sided saucepan and a watchful eye. Strawberry jam is my favourite filling, but chocolate spread, caramel and custard are also pretty awesome. Whichever you choose, make sure to be generous.

In a small cup, combine the yeast with 2 tablespoons of warm water. In a large bowl, combine the flours and salt.

In a medium saucepan, combine the milk, butter and honey. Heat gently until the butter just begins to melt, then remove from the heat and stir until completely melted. The mixture should feel warm if you insert a finger, but not hot.

Stir the beaten eggs into the milk mixture, followed by the yeast. Pour into the flour and bring together to form a wet, sticky dough. If you have a stand mixer, it's great for this recipe, otherwise tip the dough onto a lightly oiled work surface and knead for about 10 minutes until soft and smooth. The dough will feel very sticky at first, but as the gluten develops it will become smoother and silky feeling. Place the dough in a lightly oiled bowl, cover with a clean tea towel and leave in a warm, draught-free spot for an hour or until roughly doubled in size.

Lightly oil a baking tray. When the dough has risen, scrape it out of the bowl onto a lightly floured work surface. Gently roll out to about 2cm thick and use a lightly floured cutter to cut out discs of dough roughly 8cm in diameter. Re-roll and repeat with any scraps to use up all the dough, then place the discs on the lightly oiled tray, cover with a tea towel and leave to rise for a further hour.

When ready to cook the doughnuts, pour the caster sugar into a large, shallow dish. Heat the sunflower oil in a large, deep-sided saucepan. The oil should read 175°C on a thermometer – if you don't have one you can check to see if it's ready by dropping in a small scrap of dough. If it crisps up in about 30 seconds, you're good to go.

(continued)

Makes about 16 doughnuts

7g fast-action yeast
250g strong white flour
250g plain white flour, plus extra for dusting
1 tsp salt
200ml milk
50g butter, cubed
2 heaped tbsp honey
2 eggs, beaten
1.5 litres sunflower oil, to fry, plus extra for greasing
175g caster sugar, for rolling
250–300g strawberry jam, homemade (see page 239) or shop-bought

Remove the tea towel and gently and carefully drop 2 or 3 discs of risen dough away from you into the oil. Fry for 1–2 minutes on one side, or until golden, before flipping and frying for a further 2 minutes. Don't try to cook more than three at once or the oil will lose its heat.

Remove the cooked doughnuts from the pan using a slotted spoon. Drain on kitchen paper then roll in the sugar while still hot before transferring to a plate. Repeat with the remaining dough.

Allow the doughnuts to cool for a few minutes, then cut a slit in the side with a sharp knife and spoon or pipe jam into the centre of each one until it feels fat and full.

Best eaten warm, these doughnuts will keep in an airtight container for 2 days.

Homemade hint

For inside-out doughnuts, roll the dough into 32 little balls and deep-fry for about 30 seconds each side. Serve the filling alongside, for dipping.

BANOFFEE PECAN ÉCLAIRS

In amongst the latest trend of cronuts (a croissant crossed with a doughnut), townies (a tart crossed with a brownie) and duffins (you get the idea . . .), banoffee is a classic combination that has stood the test of time.

I could quite happily consume the whole batch of caramelised banoffee cream filling on its own, with a spoon, but it's even more delicious piped inside crisp choux pastry, smothered with more caramel and topped with crunchy nuts.

Makes 10–12 éclairs

For the choux pastry
125g plain white flour
60g butter, cubed
2 tsp caster sugar
pinch salt
3 eggs, lightly beaten

For the filling
15g butter
1 large banana, peeled and cut into thick rounds
2 tbsp Milk caramel (see page 246) or shop-bought dulce de leche
1 tsp vanilla extract, homemade (see page 249) or shop-bought
½ tsp ground cinnamon
pinch salt
250ml double cream

For the glaze
150g Milk caramel (see above)
50ml double cream
100g pecan halves

Preheat the oven to 200°C/180°C fan/400°F/Gas mark 6. Line two baking trays with baking parchment. Sift the flour over a third piece of baking parchment and place it close to the hob.

In a medium saucepan, combine 150ml of water with the butter, sugar and salt over a gentle heat, stirring until the butter has melted. Bring to the boil and as soon as the mixture is bubbling, tip in the flour and turn the heat down low. Vigorously beat the mixture with a wooden spoon for about 1 minute until you have a smooth dough that pulls away from the sides of the pan into a ball.

Remove from the heat and transfer the dough to a large, clean bowl. Allow to cool for 5 minutes, then use a wooden spoon or hand-held electric mixer to beat in the eggs, a little at a time, until you have a smooth, glossy dough that just about drops off the spoon.

Pipe or spoon lines of choux pastry onto the prepared baking trays, leaving a few centimetres between each one to allow the éclairs room to expand as they bake.

Bake for 20 minutes then, without opening the oven door, turn the heat down to 180°C/160°C fan/350°F/Gas mark 4 and bake for a further 15–20 minutes or until completely crisp and golden. Transfer to a wire rack and pierce the side of each one with a skewer to allow the steam to escape (this will keep them crisp). Leave to cool completely.

64

While the éclairs are baking, melt the butter for the filling in a small saucepan. Add the banana rounds, cooking for 1–2 minutes until slightly softened, then stir in the caramel. Cook for a minute more then turn off the heat and stir in the vanilla, cinnamon and salt. Allow to cool, then use the back of a fork to mash the bananas and make a smooth paste.

Whip the cream to soft peaks then fold in the cooled caramel banana mixture.

Make the glaze by whisking together the milk caramel and cream in a small bowl to a thick, but pourable consistency. If it looks too thick, whisk in a little more cream.

To assemble, slice the éclairs horizontally with a sharp knife. Pipe or spoon the banana cream onto the inside bottom of each bun, then replace the top half. Spoon the glaze over the top of each éclair and finish with the pecan halves.

Chill the éclairs until ready to eat. They are best eaten on the day of making.

LEMON AND WHITE CHOCOLATE ÉCLAIRS

Stir 2–3 tablespoons of Lemon curd (homemade, see page 244, or shop bought) into whipped cream for an alternative filling, then top with melted white chocolate.

COFFEE AND WALNUT CHOUX BUNS

Bake the choux dough as 12 large buns and fill with whipped cream once cooled. For the glaze, whisk together 140g icing sugar, 60ml double cream, 2 tablespoons maple syrup and 1 tablespoon instant espresso powder until smooth. Spoon the glaze over each bun and top with a walnut half (also pictured overleaf).

MALT WHISKY LOAF

I have deeply fond memories of eating malt loaf as a child, a dense, sticky brick thickly sliced and spread with lots of salty butter. Rich with dried fruit and whisky, this homemade version contains just enough booze to feel like a proper grown-up treat.

To achieve the holy grail of squidge, leave your loaf wrapped tightly for at least 24 hours before eating. A sensible enough instruction, it might seem, until you smell the sweet, malty notes wafting from the oven as it bakes.

Serves 8–10

For the loaf
sunflower oil, for
   greasing
160g mixed raisins and
   sultanas (prunes and
   dates will also work if
   you chop them finely)
100ml just-boiled water
50ml whisky (or
   substitute strong
   black tea for an
   alcohol-free version)
30g dark muscovado
   sugar
2 tbsp liquid malt
   extract (syrup)
1 tbsp treacle
1 egg
125g self-raising flour
¼ tsp bicarbonate of
   soda
pinch salt

For the glaze
1 tbsp liquid malt
   extract (syrup)
2 tsp whisky or strong
   black tea, as above

Preheat the oven to 150°C/130°C fan/300°F/Gas mark 2. Lightly grease a 500g loaf tin with oil and line the bottom with baking parchment.

In a medium saucepan, combine the dried fruit, water and whisky. Bring to the boil, then reduce the heat and simmer for 2 minutes until the fruit has softened slightly. Remove from the heat and stir in the sugar, malt extract and treacle.

Tip half the fruit and all its liquid into a food processor or blender. (You could also use a stick blender.) Blitz until smooth, then return to the pan with the remaining dried fruit and leave to cool for 5 minutes.

Beat in the egg then sift over the flour, bicarbonate of soda and salt. Fold quickly to combine then scrape the batter into your prepared tin. Bake for 50 minutes or until the top is firm to the touch and a skewer inserted in the middle comes out clean with just a few crumbs.

Remove the loaf from the oven and prick all over with a skewer. Gently warm the malt extract and whisky in a small saucepan then pour over the top of your loaf. Leave to cool in the tin for 5 minutes then transfer to a wire rack to cool completely.

Tightly wrap the cooled loaf in greaseproof paper then cling film and store at room temperature for 1–2 days.

Serve in slices spread with enough salty butter to leave indentations of your teeth. The loaf will keep in an airtight container for up to 1 week.

WHOLEMEAL TOASTER PASTRIES

After numerous failed attempts to convince my mum of the merits of pop tarts, my first taste at a friend's house was a total disappointment. Mass-produced pastry just doesn't compare to the crisp, flaky version you can make in your own kitchen.

Filled with homemade jam, these pastries make a perfectly acceptable breakfast. They're also brilliant warm with ice cream, for dessert. I love making heart-shapes for anniversaries or Valentine's Day, and although they're less sturdy than their shop-bought namesake, these little tarts also travel well for parties or picnics.

About an hour before you begin, wrap the butter in cling film and pop it in the freezer to get nice and cold.

In a large bowl or in a stand mixer fitted with the paddle attachment, combine the flours, sugar and salt. Grate the partially frozen butter into the flour and stir to form a crumbly mixture.

Add the vinegar and water, one tablespoon at a time, gently bringing the mixture together to form a shaggy dough (you may not need all the water). Knead the dough a couple of times to combine, but take care not to over-work it. You should have streaks of butter running through the dough. Flatten into a disc, wrap in cling film and chill for 30 minutes.

Line two baking trays with baking parchment. Remove the dough from the fridge, transfer to a lightly floured work surface and divide into two equal pieces. Roll one piece into a large rectangle roughly 3–4mm thick. Cut into 12 equal-sized rectangles then carefully place on the prepared baking trays with a few centimetres between each one.

In a small bowl, mix together the egg yolk and milk, then use a pastry brush to paint this wash round the edge of each rectangle. Don't use it all, keep some wash aside.

Spoon a scant teaspoon of jam in a thin line down the centre of each rectangle, leaving a gap of about 1cm all round the edge.

Roll out the second piece of dough to the same thickness, cut into 12 rectangles and place one on top of each jam-covered rectangle, pressing down to seal the jam inside. Crimp the edges using a fork then chill for 1 hour. This will help the pastries keep their shape when baking.

Preheat the oven to 180°C/160°C fan/350°F/Gas mark 4. Remove the chilled pastries from the fridge. Brush with the remaining egg wash, sprinkle with demerara sugar then cut three little slits in the top of each one (this will let out any steam when baking).

Bake for 20–25 minutes until golden and the filling bubbles up from the slits slightly.

These pastries are best eaten on the day of baking, but will keep in an airtight container for 2 days.

CHOCOLATE HAZELNUT TOASTER PASTRIES

Try replacing the jam with Milk chocolate hazelnut spread (see page 242) and a handful of toasted, chopped hazelnuts for a treat to rival any chocolate croissant.

Makes 12 pastries

115g butter
100g plain white flour, plus extra for dusting
100g wholemeal spelt flour (or substitute with the same amount of plain flour)
1 tbsp caster sugar
large pinch salt
1 tsp cider vinegar
3–4 tbsp iced water
1 egg yolk, to glaze
2 tsp milk, to glaze
110g of your favourite jam, homemade (see page 239) or shop-bought
4–5 tbsp demerara sugar, to sprinkle

CAKES

BECAUSE EVERY
OCCASION
IS BETTER
WITH CAKE

PINK GRAPEFRUIT, GINGER
AND POPPY-SEED CUPCAKES   76

MINI CARROT CAKES WITH
COCONUT AND LIME   78

NECTARINE AND POLENTA
UPSIDE-DOWN CAKE   80

SPICED STRAWBERRY, ORANGE
AND ALMOND LAYER CAKE   82

PISTACHIO AND LIME LOAF WITH
HONEY APRICOT DRIZZLE   84

TRIPLE CHOCOLATE CATERPILLAR CAKE   86

WHITE MODELLING CHOCOLATE   90

NUTTY, BUTTERY CRISP RICE SQUARES   91

CHOCOLATE HONEYCOMB BISCUIT CAKE   92

ONE-BOWL CHOCOLATE CAKE
WITH YOGHURT GANACHE   94

CHOCOLATE LEAVES   95

ROASTED CHERRY AND WHITE
CHOCOLATE BROWNIES   98

COCONUT AND RASPBERRY BATTENBERG   100

COCONUT MARZIPAN   104

CHOCOLATE-FRECKLED BANANA BREAD   105

As long as I can remember, I've made my own birthday cake, starting with a tin in the shape of a 'K' and progressing on to more elaborate designs. My mum's signature chocolate cake with yoghurt ganache was perhaps the most regular in rotation, but I can clearly remember several years when only a variation of the chocolate biscuit cake on page 92 would do.

Homemade cakes are a wonderful thing to make for friends and family. I've taken them to birthdays at restaurants and nightclubs, on my lap in taxis and across London on the tube. It's wonderful to see peoples' faces light up, not just at the cake itself but the effort that goes into making it. Having made, shared and eaten enough in my lifetime, I can safely say that a slightly lopsided creation baked with a little love is worth a dozen perfect shop-bought versions.

In the words of Julia Child, 'a party without cake is just a meeting'. But cake is a pretty great thing to bring to a meeting too. This chapter includes the cakes I love making most for all kinds of occasions, from a show-stopping chocolate caterpillar to simple cupcakes and my absolute favourite brownies.

PINK GRAPEFRUIT, GINGER AND POPPY-SEED CUPCAKES

With their citrus scented sponge and sticky ginger syrup, I'd take one of these little cakes over their sparkly, buttercream-clad counterparts any day. Pink grapefruit is a lovely alternative to lemon in baking with a tangy, bittersweet flavour and plenty of juice. If you fancy doubling the quantity, the gingery syrup can be topped up with champagne to make a refreshing, slightly spicy cocktail. Cheers!

Makes 12 cupcakes

For the cakes
175g plain white flour
1 tsp baking powder
175g caster sugar
175g softened butter,
   cubed
3 eggs, lightly beaten
finely grated zest of
   1 pink grapefruit
½ tsp ground ginger
1 tbsp poppy seeds

For the syrup
100ml pink grapefruit
   juice
80g caster sugar
25g fresh root ginger,
   peel on, sliced

For the icing
150g icing sugar, sifted
2–3 tsp pink grapefruit
   juice
12 pieces crystallised
   ginger, to decorate
   (optional)

Preheat the oven to 180°C/160°C fan/350°F/Gas mark 4. Line a 12-hole muffin tin with paper or silicone cases.

In a large bowl, sift together the flour and baking powder. Add the sugar, butter, eggs, grapefruit zest and ginger and beat to combine. You can also do this in a stand mixer or food processor. Fold in the poppy seeds.

Divide the mixture between the prepared cases. Bake for 17–20 minutes until risen and golden: the cupcakes should feel springy to the touch. Remove from the oven and leave to cool in the tin for 5 minutes then transfer to a wire rack to cool completely.

While the cupcakes are baking, make the syrup. In a small saucepan, combine the grapefruit juice, sugar and ginger. Bring to the boil then reduce the heat and simmer for 3–4 minutes until slightly thickened. Remove from the heat, strain through a fine mesh sieve and set aside to cool slightly.

Use a skewer to poke holes in the top of each still-warm cupcake and paint over the gingery syrup with a pastry brush. Be generous: the cakes will soak up the syrup, making them moist and full of flavour.

To make the icing, combine the icing sugar and grapefruit juice in a medium bowl, whisking until smooth. Add a little more juice, if necessary, to achieve the consistency you'd like. Spoon a little icing over the top of each cake, top with a piece of ginger (if using) then leave for 30 minutes to firm up at room temperature.

The iced cupcakes will keep in an airtight container for 2–3 days.

MINI CARROT CAKES
WITH COCONUT AND LIME

One day at primary school I opened my lunchbox to find a pair of gnarly organic carrots, foot-long green fronds intact. My mum had included them in my packed lunch and the Bugs Bunny jokes from my school friends lasted for weeks.

Grated into tender, coconutty cupcakes, carrots make for a much more acceptable lunchtime treat. The only greenery here comes from a sprinkling of lime zest and pistachios on top.

Makes 12 cakes

For the cakes
125g wholemeal flour
1 tsp baking powder
¼ tsp bicarbonate of
    soda
1 tsp ground cinnamon
pinch freshly grated
    nutmeg
pinch salt
50g unsweetened
    desiccated coconut
2 eggs
110g dark muscovado
    sugar
1 tbsp golden syrup
90ml groundnut or
    vegetable oil
175g carrots (about 2
    medium), peeled and
    grated
finely grated zest of half
    an orange

For the icing
100g butter, softened
100g cream cheese
250g icing sugar
finely grated zest of
    1 small lime
30g pistachio nuts,
    roughly chopped

Preheat the oven to 180°C/160°C fan/350°F/Gas mark 4. Line a 12-hole muffin tin with paper or silicone cases.

In a medium bowl, sift together the flour, baking powder, bicarbonate of soda, spices and salt. Stir in the desiccated coconut and any excess bran from the sieve.

In a separate medium bowl with a hand-held electric mixer, or in a stand mixer, whisk the eggs, sugar, golden syrup and oil together for 4–5 minutes until thick and almost doubled in volume. Gently fold in the dry ingredients, taking care not to knock out too much volume, then fold in the grated carrot and orange zest.

Spoon the mixture into the cases about two thirds full and bake for 20 minutes or until risen and a skewer inserted in the middle comes out almost clean. Remove from the oven, leave to cool in the tin for 5 minutes then transfer to a wire rack to cool completely.

To make the icing, beat the butter for 1 minute then beat in the cream cheese until smooth and light. Sift over the icing sugar and beat slowly until combined, then turn up the speed and beat for a further 1 minute until really light and fluffy. Fold in the lime zest, transfer to a piping bag and pipe swirls of icing on top of each cooled cake. Sprinkle over the pistachios.

Once iced, eat within 2 days. The un-iced cakes will keep in an airtight container for 4–5 days.

NECTARINE AND POLENTA UPSIDE-DOWN CAKE

My dad likes to talk and think about food as much as I love to cook it. Rarely a day goes by without us discussing what we've eaten and he often sends me recipes he thinks I'd like to make (or make for him). Polenta cake is one of his absolute favourites.

With an upside-down topping and moist, sandy texture, this charmingly retro cake is naturally gluten free. If you're baking for someone who is sensitive to gluten, make sure to use gluten-free baking powder.

Preheat the oven to 190°C/170°C fan/375°F/Gas mark 5. Lightly grease a 20cm round cake tin with butter and line the bottom with baking parchment. Generously grease the parchment with butter too. It's best not to use a loose-bottomed tin here, but if that's all you have, tightly wrap a double layer of aluminium foil around the outside of the base to prevent any juices escaping.

Quarter the nectarines and cut them into thin slices. Toss with the sugar and lemon juice then arrange in a single layer, slightly overlapping, round the bottom of your tin. Scrape any excess sugar syrup over the top.

To make the sponge, cream the butter and sugar in a medium bowl with a wooden spoon, or in a stand mixer fitted with the paddle attachment, until light and fluffy. Add the eggs, a little at a time, beating well between each addition. Fold in the almonds, polenta, baking powder, lemon zest and salt.

Spoon the batter over the nectarines, smooth the surface with a spatula then tap firmly on the work surface to remove any bubbles. Bake for 35–40 minutes or until risen and golden.

Remove the cake from the oven, run a sharp knife round the edge then leave to cool for 10 minutes before turning out onto a plate.

Serve warm or at room temperature.

The cake will keep in an airtight container for 2–3 days.

Serves 6–8

For the topping
2 medium nectarines
  – or equal quantity
  of other stone fruit
  – skin on, stones
  removed
75g light muscovado
  sugar
juice of half a lemon

For the sponge
120g butter, softened,
  plus extra for
  greasing
125g caster sugar
2 eggs, lightly beaten
75g ground almonds
75g fine or 'quick cook'
  polenta
1 tsp baking powder
finely grated zest of
  1 lemon
pinch salt

SPICED STRAWBERRY, ORANGE AND ALMOND LAYER CAKE

When it comes to birthdays, a simple Victoria sponge is hard to beat. It might not come with fancy icing or multiple layers, but that's all part of the appeal. Rather than the traditional, slightly austere scraping of jam, my version is sandwiched together with strawberries macerated in a sticky spiced jam and a good inch of softly whipped cream. I like the slight sharpness of cream cut with yoghurt, but do use an extra 50ml double cream, if you prefer.

Preheat the oven to 190°C/170°C fan/375°F/Gas mark 5. Grease two 20cm round loose-bottomed cake tins with butter and line the bases with baking parchment. Sift the flour and baking powder into a medium bowl, holding the sieve up high to aerate the mixture.

In a large bowl with a wooden spoon, or in a stand mixer fitted with the paddle attachment, cream the butter for 2–3 minutes until light and fluffy. Add the sugar and beat for another minute or two. Add the eggs a little at a time, along with 1–2 teaspoons of flour per egg, mixing well between each addition. This should prevent the mixture from curdling, but don't panic if it does: the cake will still taste good.

Gently fold in the remaining flour, ground almonds and orange zest, followed by the milk until you have a uniform, smooth mixture that drops easily from the spoon – you may not need all the milk.

Divide the mixture between the two prepared tins and gently smooth the surface of each one. Bake for 20–25 minutes or until risen and golden: the tops should feel springy to the touch and a skewer inserted in the middle should come out clean. Remove from the oven, leave to cool in the tins for 5 minutes then transfer to a wire rack to cool completely.

While the cakes are baking, make the filling. In a medium saucepan, combine the jam, orange zest and juice and all the spices except the vanilla, and warm over a low heat for 1 minute or until the jam has loosened slightly. Add the strawberries, stirring to coat with the jam, then remove from the heat and leave to cool completely.

Remove the star anise from the strawberries and stir in the vanilla seeds. In a medium bowl, whip the cream until soft peaks form and fold in the Greek yoghurt.

Place one of the cooled cakes on a serving plate or stand and spread with the cream. Top with the spiced strawberries, then place the second cake on top. Dust with icing sugar and serve in thick slices.

Once filled, this cake should be eaten the same day. The plain sponges will keep in an airtight container for up to 2 days.

Serves 8–10

For the sponge
175g self-raising flour
2 tsp baking powder
225g butter, softened and cubed, plus extra for greasing
225g caster sugar
4 medium eggs, lightly beaten
50g ground almonds
finely grated zest of 1 orange
1–2 tbsp milk

For the filling
90g strawberry jam, homemade (see page 239) or shop-bought
1 tsp finely grated orange zest
2 tsp orange juice
1 star anise
½ tsp ground cinnamon
pinch ground ginger
pinch ground cardamom
pinch freshly grated nutmeg
225g fresh strawberries, hulled and quartered
seeds of half a vanilla pod
200ml double cream
50g Greek yoghurt

icing sugar, for dusting

PISTACHIO AND LIME LOAF WITH HONEY APRICOT DRIZZLE

A citrus loaf is a very lovely thing. Lemon drizzle tends to steal the limelight, but I love the tangy taste of lime zest and its slightly sweeter juice. Here, the addition of ground pistachio nuts makes for a rich, moist loaf with a beautiful, jewel-like topping.

Serves 8–10

For the cake
65g shelled pistachio
   nuts
125g self-raising flour
pinch salt
175g butter, softened,
   plus extra for
   greasing
175g caster sugar
finely grated zest of
   3 limes
3 eggs, lightly beaten
1–2 tbsp milk

For the glaze
65g dried apricots,
   roughly chopped
2 tbsp honey
juice of 3 limes
40g pistachio nuts,
   roughly chopped with
   a sharp knife

Preheat the oven to 170°C/150°C fan/335°F/Gas mark 3. Grease a 1kg loaf tin with butter and line with baking parchment.

Blitz the pistachio nuts to a fine powder in a food processor. Transfer to a bowl then sift over the flour and salt, stirring to combine.

In a medium bowl, cream together the butter and sugar. Add the lime zest and cream for a further 3–4 minutes until really pale and fluffy.

Beat in the eggs, a little at a time, adding a teaspoonful of the flour mixture with each addition. Then, fold in the remaining flour and pistachio mixture until just combined. Fold in a little milk until the mixture drops gently off your spoon: you may not need all the milk.

Scrape the batter into the prepared tin, smooth the top and bake for 55–60 minutes until risen, golden and firm to the touch. A skewer inserted in the middle should come out fairly clean with a few crumbs still clinging to it as this is a moist cake.

Remove from the oven and run a knife around the edges of the cake. Allow to cool in the tin for 10 minutes.

To make the syrup, combine the apricots, honey and lime juice in a small saucepan. Bring to a simmer then cook for 3–4 minutes until the apricots have softened and the mixture is slightly thicker and syrupy. Stir in the pistachios.

Transfer the cake from its tin to a wire rack. Poke holes in the top with a skewer then pour over the warm syrup, evenly distributing the pistachios and apricots. Leave to cool completely then serve in thick slices.

The glazed cake will keep in an airtight container for 4–5 days.

TRIPLE CHOCOLATE CATERPILLAR CAKE

Once the preserve of children's birthday parties, chocolate caterpillar cake has achieved something of a cult status amongst the adults I know. This homemade version might look complicated but the component parts couldn't be easier: a one-bowl chocolate sponge, hazelnut whipped cream and a three-ingredient chocolate coating that cuts with a satisfying crack.

Serves 8–10

To decorate
White modelling chocolate (see page 90) or shop-bought (see Suppliers, page 13)
coloured chocolate buttons (such as Smarties)

For the sponge
5 eggs
100g caster sugar
60g plain white flour
40g cocoa powder
1 tsp vanilla extract, homemade (see page 249) or shop-bought
1 tbsp icing sugar, for dusting
1 tbsp Frangelico (optional)
sunflower oil, for greasing

For the filling
200ml double cream
100g Milk chocolate hazelnut spread (see page 242) or shop-bought chocolate spread

Start by making the caterpillar face and feet with the white modelling chocolate. Divide the chocolate into one third and two thirds. Roll the larger piece into a ball then flatten into a disc, pinching at the top to create a face shape. Press in two brown chocolate buttons to create eyes and a pink one for the mouth. Divide the remaining chocolate into eight balls and shape into feet. Set aside in a cool place.

Preheat the oven to 180°C/160°C fan/350°F/Gas mark 4. Lightly grease a Swiss roll tin approximately 20 x 30cm and line with baking parchment, making sure it comes up at least 2.5cm above the edge of the rim. Tear off a sheet of aluminium foil double the size of your Swiss roll tin.

In a medium bowl, whisk the eggs with a hand-held electric mixer for 1–2 minutes until they begin to thicken. Add the sugar and continue whisking for 4–5 minutes until pale and thick (the mixture should fall off your whisk in ribbons). Sift over the flour and cocoa and fold in along with the vanilla.

Pour into the prepared tin and bake for 12–14 minutes until a skewer inserted in the middle comes out clean. Remove from the oven and immediately wrap the tin in aluminium foil, making sure it doesn't touch the cake itself and taking care not to burn yourself or let out any heat. This will trap in steam and make the cake easier to roll once cooled. Set aside to cool completely.

For the filling, whip the cream and chocolate hazelnut spread in a medium bowl, until fairly firm peaks form. You don't want the cream to stiffen but it needs to be slightly firmer than you'd usually whip cream to help the cake hold its shape.

(continued)

Lay a piece of cling film about 30 x 40cm out on the work surface and cover with a piece of baking parchment the same size. Dust lightly with icing sugar. Turn the cooled cake onto the baking parchment and use a pastry brush to brush over the Frangelico (if using).

Spread the chocolate cream over the cake in an even layer, leaving a margin of about 2cm all the way round. Using the baking parchment to guide you, roll up the cake as tightly as you can, starting from the long side. Make sure the seam is underneath the cake then wrap it tightly in the cling film and place in the freezer for 1 hour, to firm up.

Ten minutes before you take the cake out of the freezer, prepare the coating. Melt the chocolates and butter in a heat-proof bowl suspended over a pan of barely simmering water (make sure that the bowl doesn't touch the water), stirring until smooth and glossy. Remove from the heat and set aside to cool for 5 minutes.

Place a strip of baking parchment approximately 30 x 10cm on a board that will fit in your fridge. Unwrap the cake and slice a 3cm thick piece from one end. Cut that piece in half to create two semi-circles of cake. Cut one of these semi-circles in half again. Press the larger semi-circle against the cut end of the cake, flat side against the board. Press one of the quarter circles against this to create the caterpillar tail. Eat or discard the remaining quarter.

Spoon the melted chocolate over the cake, ensuring the whole cake is coated. Chill for 2–3 minutes to firm up the chocolate slightly then use a palette knife to scrape away any excess. Press the chocolate caterpillar face into the opposite end from the tail, press the feet down each side and decorate with coloured chocolate buttons. Chill until ready to serve.

The decorated cake will keep in the fridge for 2–3 days.

For the coating
140g milk chocolate,
    roughly chopped
140g dark chocolate,
    roughly chopped
30g butter, cubed

WHITE MODELLING CHOCOLATE

Made with golden syrup, this is infinitely more delicious than the pre-made versions you can buy. The secret to success is to combine the chocolate and syrup at roughly the same temperature: if either ingredient is too hot or too cold, the mixture can split. I use a microwave, to provide short bursts of heat, and good quality white chocolate. Green and Black's or Menier Chocolat Patissier both work well.

195g white chocolate, 30 per cent minimum cocoa butter, roughly chopped
3 tbsp golden syrup

Homemade hint

If the chocolate feels greasy, don't panic, it can be rescued. Chill for 30 minutes then knead gently – it should come back together.

Place the chocolate in a heat-proof bowl. Microwave on high for 30 seconds then stir. Microwave for a further 30 seconds then stir continuously until any lumps are completely melted and the mixture is smooth. Don't be tempted to microwave it again – you don't want to overheat the chocolate.

In a small heat-proof jug, microwave the golden syrup for 30 seconds. You want it about the same temperature as the chocolate otherwise the cocoa butter will split out of the chocolate and make it too greasy to use (see hint).

Pour the golden syrup into the chocolate, stirring gently with a rubber spatula to combine. The mixture will thicken considerably, pulling away from the sides of the bowl. Stir until just combined then stop: over-mixing will cause the chocolate to split.

Lay a piece of cling film on the work surface and scrape the chocolate onto the centre. Flatten slightly so you have a rectangular shape about 1cm thick, wrap the cling film round it and leave to firm up completely at room temperature. This can take 2–6 hours, depending how warm your room is.

When the chocolate is firm, break off a small piece and knead it with your hands until it becomes smooth and pliable. If it feels too firm, microwave in bursts of 5 seconds until just soft enough to knead.

The chocolate will keep in an airtight container for up to 3 weeks.

NUTTY, BUTTERY CRISP RICE SQUARES

Straightforward, sticky, one-bowl fun, crispy rice cereal treats are one of the first recipes I learned to make as a child. Here you get a double hit of nuttiness from toasty brown butter and peanut butter, the two tangled together in a chewy goo of marshmallowy goodness then drizzled with chocolate.

These squares tastes best made with plain marshmallows, so if you're making your own, follow the instructions on page 204 and omit the peppermint extract.

Lightly grease a 20cm square cake tin with butter and line the base with baking parchment.

In a large, heavy-bottomed saucepan, brown the butter (see page 10). Reduce the heat to low and stir in the marshmallows followed by the peanut butter and salt. Once everything has melted into a smooth, gooey mess (there will be some brown speckles from the caramelised milk solids in the butter but don't worry – unless they are burnt they will taste delicious), remove from the heat and stir in the crisp rice cereal.

Scrape into the prepared tin, pressing down firmly with the back of your spatula. This will ensure each slice has a chewy, close-packed texture.

Melt the chocolate in a heat-proof bowl suspended over a pan of barely simmering water (make sure that the bowl doesn't touch the water), or in the microwave, melting in short bursts and stirring well between each one to prevent catching or burning. Drizzle the melted chocolate over the crisp rice mixture, then set aside to firm up at room temperature for about 1 hour. Remove from the tin and use a very sharp knife to slice into squares.

The rice squares are best eaten within a day of making.

Makes 16 squares

125g butter, plus extra for greasing
325g marshmallows, homemade (see page 204) or shop-bought
125g smooth peanut butter, homemade (see page 204) or shop-bought
pinch salt
160g crisp rice cereal
50g dark chocolate

CHOCOLATE HONEYCOMB BISCUIT CAKE

My big brother Max has always loved cooking. When we were both very young, he was given a book called Keep Out of the Kitchen Mum _and together we spent hours recreating recipes from its pages without any adult interference._

One of the recipes was for chocolate refrigerator cake: a simple, no-bake cake made from chocolate, biscuits and butter. As children, we'd triple the recipe to fill a giant rabbit-shaped birthday cake mould and serve it on a 'field' of wobbly green jelly. For everyday eating, this loaf-shaped cake is a little more practical.

Makes 10 very rich slices

125g butter, plus extra for greasing
350g dark chocolate, roughly chopped
1 generous tbsp golden syrup
150g Wholemeal spelt digestives (see page 21) or shop-bought digestive biscuits
75g Real honeycomb (see page 197) or shop-bought honeycomb
1 egg, lightly beaten
50g pecans, roughly chopped
1–2 tbsp cocoa powder, for dusting

Lightly grease a 1kg loaf tin with butter then line with baking parchment making sure it comes a few centimetres above the edges.

In a large bowl suspended over a pan of barely simmering water, melt the chocolate, butter and golden syrup, stirring until smooth. Remove from the heat and set aside to cool slightly.

Place the biscuits in a large bowl and use the end of a rolling pin to gently bash them into rough pieces: you want a mixture of chunks of biscuit and large crumbs. Add the honeycomb and bash again.

Pasteurise the egg by stirring it slowly and continuously into the chocolate mixture. Stir in the biscuits, honeycomb and pecans until well combined. Scrape the mixture into the prepared tin, levelling it with a spatula. Press a piece of baking parchment over the top then chill in the fridge for about 4 hours or until firm.

Remove the cake from the fridge 10 minutes before serving to allow it to soften slightly. Turn it out of the tin, dust the top with cocoa powder then serve in thick slices.

The cake will keep in the fridge for up to 1 week.

VARIATION

Substitute the digestive biscuits with the same quantity of Oaty dunkers (see page 22) or Spiced gingerbread (see page 42) and add a handful of different nuts or dried fruit.

ONE-BOWL CHOCOLATE CAKE WITH YOGHURT GANACHE

Everyone needs a one-bowl chocolate cake in the bank: something delicious that can be thrown together in minutes with minimal washing up. Tender and delicately chocolaty rather than fudgy, this is the one we'd make with my mum as children, for birthdays and parties and simply because.

Until the age of about 15 I don't think I'd ever made buttercream as we always iced our cakes with chocolate and yoghurt: the two combined to make a firm, tangy icing. Decorate the cake with Chocolate leaves (see opposite) or as is if you prefer.

Serves 8

For the cake
3 tbsp cocoa powder
125g plain white flour
2 tsp baking powder
150g butter, softened and cubed, plus extra for greasing
150g caster sugar
25g light muscovado sugar
3 eggs, lightly beaten
1 tsp vanilla extract, homemade (see page 249) or shop-bought
pinch salt

For the yoghurt ganache
200g dark chocolate, chopped
1 tbsp golden syrup
125g natural yoghurt

Preheat the oven to 190°C/170°C fan/375°F/Gas mark 5. Lightly grease a 20cm round loose-bottomed cake tin with butter and line the base with baking parchment.

Sift the cocoa powder into a large bowl. Add 3 tablespoons of warm water and whisk until smooth. Sift over the flour and baking powder then add the butter, sugars, eggs, vanilla and salt and beat until just combined. You can also do this in a stand mixer, or a food processor.

Scrape the batter into the prepared tin and bake for 35–40 minutes, or until a skewer inserted in the middle comes out clean. Remove from the oven and leave to cool in the tin for 5–10 minutes then transfer to a wire rack to cool completely. Once cool, slice the cake in half horizontally using a serrated knife and place the bottom half on a serving plate or board.

To make the ganache, melt the chocolate and golden syrup in a heat-proof bowl suspended over a pan of simmering water (make sure that the bowl doesn't touch the water). Remove from the heat and leave to cool for 6–8 minutes. Fold in the yoghurt until just combined – it will stiffen if you over-fold – then quickly spread one third over the bottom half of the sponge. Place the second sponge on top, then spread over the remaining ganache, using a palette knife to smooth. Decorate with chocolate leaves, if you like, then allow to set at room temperature.

The iced cake will keep in an airtight container for 2–3 days.

CHOCOLATE LEAVES

When I was younger I'd make dozens of these leaves to decorate birthday cakes in dark, milk and white chocolate. They look wonderfully impressive but are quick and easy to make. Any leaf with a prominent stem and veins works well: I use rose or mint leaves from the garden. Just make sure not to pick anything poisonous: death by chocolate isn't quite what's intended here!

Carefully wash the leaves under running water then pat dry on a tea towel. Melt the chocolate in a heat-proof bowl suspended over a pan of simmering water (make sure that the bowl doesn't touch the water) or in the microwave, melting in short bursts and stirring well between each burst to prevent catching or burning, then remove from the heat and set aside to cool for 2–3 minutes. Alternatively, follow the instructions for tempering chocolate on page 188 to give the leaves extra snap and shine.

Line a small tray with baking parchment. Using a teaspoon, carefully spoon a thick layer of chocolate on the veiny underside of each leaf. Place, chocolate side up, on the prepared tray, until all the chocolate is used up, then chill for about 10 minutes until firm.

Remove the tray from the fridge and carefully peel the leaves away from the chocolate. If your hands are unsteady, use a pair of tweezers to tease them off.

The chocolate leaves will keep in an airtight container in the fridge for up to 1 week.

Makes about
20 leaves

about 20 freshly picked leaves
200g dark, milk or white chocolate, chopped

ROASTED CHERRY AND WHITE CHOCOLATE BROWNIES

. . . .

On a piece of paper at my parents' house, tucked inside a dog-eared edition of a Mrs Beeton cookbook, there's a handwritten recipe for brownies. Covered in chocolaty fingerprints, it pays testament to the recipe I've baked most often in my life: most memorably, the first time my new boyfriend visited me at university. It's hard to improve on perfection, but here I've added creamy white chocolate and juicy roasted cherries. Leave these brownies plain if you prefer – that boyfriend is now my husband, so I'd say the original recipe is a winner.

Preheat the oven to 200°C/180°C fan/400°F/Gas mark 6. Grease a 23cm square cake tin with butter then line with baking parchment.

Toss the cherries with 1 teaspoon of caster sugar and roast in a small pan for 15–20 minutes until they just begin to soften. Set aside to cool completely then cut in half and squeeze out the stones. Strain off any excess juice and discard.

Reduce the oven temperature to 170°C/150°C fan/335°F/Gas mark 3. In a heat-proof bowl suspended over a pan of barely simmering water (make sure that the bowl doesn't touch the water), melt the chocolate and butter. Set aside to cool for 5 minutes.

In a separate bowl, whisk together the eggs, remaining caster sugar, muscovado sugar and vanilla for 1 minute. Add the cooled chocolate mixture and whisk for 3 minutes until glossy and combined. This will help give the brownies their shiny, tissue-thin crust.

Sift over the flour, cocoa powder and salt and fold to combine. Fold in the cherries and white chocolate then scrape the mixture into your prepared tin.

Bake for 27–32 minutes or until the top is set firm and a skewer inserted at the edge comes out with a few crumbs still clinging to it. The brownies will continue to cook once removed from the oven so it's best to err on the side of caution and take them out when slightly underdone. Leave to cool completely in the tin – if you attempt to slice sooner you'll end up with a molten chocolate mess.

Once completely cool, turn out of the tin, remove the baking parchment and slice into neat squares with a warm knife.

The brownies will keep in an airtight container for 4–5 days.

Makes 16 brownies

200g cherries, de-stalked
155g caster sugar
185g dark chocolate, roughly chopped
200g butter, plus extra for greasing
3 eggs
100g light muscovado sugar
2 tsp vanilla extract, homemade (see page 249) or shop-bought
95g plain white flour
1 tbsp cocoa powder
pinch salt
100g white chocolate, chopped into bite-sized chunks

Homemade hint

If your first batch of brownies comes out too squidgy, chill for 3 hours until firm enough to slice; if you have over-baked brownies, they can be crumbled into ice cream. If either happens, take note and adjust the baking time for your next batch accordingly: getting to know your oven is the key to consistently perfect brownies.

COCONUT AND RASPBERRY BATTENBERG

Making your own cakes is a great way to avoid nasty artificial food colourings. This Battenberg gets its delicate pastel hue from puréed raspberries, sandwiched together with lashings of homemade jam. The whole thing tastes a bit like a giant Australian lamington, wrapped tight in a blanket of coconut marzipan.

Serves 8–10

For the cake
coconut oil or butter, for
    greasing
50g fresh raspberries
4 tbsp coconut milk (or
    substitute regular
    milk)
250g plain white flour
2 tsp baking powder
50g unsweetened
    desiccated coconut
finely grated zest of
    1 lemon
pinch salt
170ml vegetable oil
260g caster sugar
3 eggs
2 tsp coconut extract

Preheat the oven to 190°C/170°C fan/375°F/Gas mark 5. Lightly grease a 20cm square Battenberg tin with coconut oil or butter. If you don't have a Battenberg tin, you'll need to divide a regular 20cm square tin in two. To do this, cut out a piece of foil-lined baking parchment to 30 x 20cm. Fold in half to make a square, then make a 5cm fold down the closed side to make a pleat in the middle. Open the parchment out and pinch the pleat so it stands upright. Use this to line the bottom of your tin with the pleat sitting upright along the middle.

In a small food processor or blender, whizz the raspberries with 2 tablespoons of the coconut milk until smooth. Press through a fine mesh sieve to remove the seeds. In a separate bowl, sift together the flour and baking powder, then stir in the desiccated coconut, lemon zest and salt.

Whisk together the oil, sugar and eggs for about 2 minutes until pale and thick. Whisk in the coconut extract. Weigh the mixture into a second bowl, then transfer half that weight back into the original bowl. Whisk 2 tablespoons of the raspberry purée into one bowl and 2 tablespoons of coconut milk into the other.

Spoon the coconut batter into one half of the tin and the raspberry batter into the other, making sure your parchment divider is still in the middle or you'll end up with lopsided cakes.

Bake for 30–35 minutes or until springy to the touch and a skewer inserted in the middle of each cake comes out clean.

(continued)

Remove the tin from the oven and run a knife round the side of each cake. Leave to cool in the tin for 10 minutes then transfer to a wire rack to cool completely.

Use a serrated knife to level the top of each cake then stack one on top of the other. Trim the sides and edges level then slice into four long strips of equal length and width. In a small bowl, stir the jam until loose and spreadable.

Lay a piece of cling film on the work surface. Spread the long side of one coconut cake strip with jam then press one raspberry strip alongside it. Place on the cling film then repeat with the two remaining strips of cake, stacking the pairs of sponge on top of one another to create a chequerboard effect. Wrap tightly in the cling film and freeze while you roll out the marzipan.

On a clean, dry work surface, roll the marzipan out between two large pieces of cling film, to a large rectangle approximately 25 x 35cm. Remove the cake from the freezer and unwrap. Brush one long side of cake with jam then place, jam side down, on the marzipan. Brush jam all over the rest of the cake and wrap the marzipan tightly around it, using the cling film to guide you. Trim each end with a sharp knife to neaten.

Use a little more raspberry jam to stick fresh raspberries in a line down the middle of the cake, then serve in dainty slices.

The cake will keep in an airtight container for 2–3 days.

To finish
175g seedless raspberry jam, homemade using raspberries instead of strawberries (see page 239) or shop-bought
icing sugar, for dusting
1 x quantity Coconut marzipan (see page 104) or 500g shop-bought marzipan
handful fresh raspberries, to decorate

COCONUT MARZIPAN

As a little girl, I was a notoriously fussy eater. At Christmas I'd always ask for a large slice of cake then carefully remove the sweet fondant icing to eat, leaving the marzipan and fruit part intact. Ever since I discovered homemade marzipan, there's no chance of that happening: it's utterly irresistible.

Makes about 550g

300g caster sugar
200g ground almonds
1 egg white
2 tsp coconut extract
icing sugar, for dusting
**   and rolling**

Homemade hint

To make marzipan sweets, omit the coconut extract and colour with a few drops of natural food colouring. Shape into fruit, top with nuts or dip in melted chocolate and you've got a simple plate of petits fours.

Make an ice water bath by filling a large bowl big enough to hold your saucepan with cold water and a handful of ice cubes. Alternatively, you could use the sink.

Gently heat the sugar with 150ml water in a heavy-bottomed saucepan until the sugar has dissolved. Turn up the heat and bring to the boil, cooking until the mixture reaches 114°C on a sugar thermometer. As soon as the mixture reaches temperature, plunge the pan into the ice water bath to stop the sugar cooking.

Stir in the ground almonds followed by the egg white then return the pan to a medium-low heat. Cook, stirring continuously, for 2–3 minutes until the marzipan begins to thicken slightly, then remove from the heat and add the coconut extract. Leave to cool for 10–15 minutes in the pan. At this stage the mixture will look quite lumpy and loose.

Liberally dust a clean work surface with icing sugar. Scrape the marzipan onto the work surface and knead until smooth and combined. Like bread dough, at first it will be sticky and difficult to work with, but after 5 or 6 minutes you should have a smooth, firm marzipan. If you have a dough scraper, this will help with the first few messy minutes.

Use immediately or wrap in cling film and chill for up to 1 week. Allow to come to room temperature again before using.

CHOCOLATE-FRECKLED BANANA BREAD

In between school and university, I spent six months as a waitress. The restaurant where I worked made the most incredible banana bread and whenever someone ordered it, I'd sneak an extra sliver for myself.

This recipe is everything I remember from those stolen mouthfuls, fudgy from muscovado sugar with freckles of dark chocolate throughout. I sometimes fold a handful of cocoa nibs or chopped walnuts into the batter for extra texture, both of which are banana's best friends.

Preheat the oven to 180°C/160°C fan/350°F/Gas mark 4. Lightly grease a 1kg loaf tin with butter and line with baking parchment.

In a medium bowl, whisk the eggs and sugar until pale and thick. Whisk in the cooled melted butter followed by the yoghurt and mashed banana: your mixture will look slightly lumpy.

Sift over the flours, baking powder and bicarbonate of soda, tipping in any bran left in the sieve, then fold to combine. Fold in the chocolate.

Scrape into the prepared tin, sprinkle with demerara sugar and bake for 1 hour or until the top is firm and golden and a skewer inserted in the middle comes out clean.

Remove from the oven and run a knife round the edge of the cake. Leave to cool in the tin for 10 minutes then transfer to a wire rack to cool completely.

This cake is delicious sliced thick and spread with Peanut butter (see page 238). It will keep in an airtight container for 4–5 days.

Serves 8–10

65g butter, melted and cooled, plus extra for greasing
2 eggs
150g light muscovado sugar
3 tbsp Greek yoghurt
300g ripe banana, roughly mashed (3–4 medium bananas)
165g wholemeal flour
25g plain white flour
1 tsp baking powder
½ tsp bicarbonate of soda
85g dark chocolate, chopped into fine shards
1 tbsp demerara sugar, for sprinkling

WHAT'S FOR PUDDING?

· · · · · · · · · · ·

COMFORT SERVED UP IN A BOWL WITH A SPOON

· · · · · · · · · ·

BLUEBERRY, ALMOND AND PLUM CRUMBLE   110

RHUBARB JELLY AND ICE CREAM
WITH CARDAMOM CRUNCH   112

BUTTERSCOTCH DEVIL'S DELIGHT   114

BRITISH SUMMER MESS   116

UPSIDE-DOWN LEMON MERINGUE PIE   119

CHEAT'S CRÈME CARAMEL WITH
CHAMOMILE AND HONEY   120

COCONUT BROWN RICE PUDDING   124

CARAMELISED RICE PUDDING POTS   126

FIG AND HAZELNUT BREAD
AND BUTTER PUDDING   128

STICKY DATE PUDDINGS
WITH COCONUT CARAMEL   130

GOOSEBERRY FOOL   132

APRICOT, JAM AND AMARETTO TART   134

PEAR AND PECAN TREACLE TART   138

BOOZY CHOCOLATE PUDDLE PUDDINGS   141

CHOCOLATE MOUSSE WITH
CAPPUCCINO CREAM   142

WHAT'S FOR PUDDING?

An amazing woman in many ways, my granny on my mother's side was not a brilliant baker. Nonetheless she understood the importance of adding a sense of occasion to the end of a meal and would always answer our cries of 'what's for pudding?' with a tantalising 'wait and see'.

As children, my brother and I were only allowed something sweet if we'd eaten up our main, which only added to the sense of excitement and anticipation. You'd think all these years later I'd have lost that thrill, but I still find pudding completely magical. Just one spoonful of crumble and I'm six years old again, running a finger round my bowl when I think nobody's looking and wondering if it's too soon to ask for seconds.

Puddings are all about comfort, but there's still room for sophistication without compromising on flavour. Inspired by happy hours spent licking the utensils from a bowl of chocolaty cake batter, my boozy chocolate puddle puddings make the perfect dinner party dessert while a caramelised crust adds elegance to that nursery staple, rice pudding.

The sure sign of a good pudding is a full belly and an empty bowl. So grab yourself a spoon and get stuck in.

BLUEBERRY, ALMOND AND PLUM CRUMBLE

———— • • • • • • • •

The day my dad brought his apple-phobic girlfriend home to the apple farm he grew up on, my granny said she knew they'd end up married. They did, but despite decades of offering my mum every apple-based dessert under the sun, Granny never managed to convert her.

Made with blueberries and plums beneath a nutty, buttery crust, this crumble is a delicious alternative to the traditional apple version. It's also close to my idea of pudding perfection and endlessly comforting, covered in custard or served with a scoop of ice cream.

Serves 6

For the fruit
350g blueberries
475g plums (about 6),
    stoned and sliced into
    3cm chunks
1 tbsp light muscovado
    sugar (you may need
    more if the fruit is
    very tart)
1 tbsp cornflour
juice of 1 lemon

For the crumble
100g plain or
    wholemeal flour
90g cold butter, cubed
85g rolled oats
65g light muscovado
    sugar
50g whole almonds,
    roughly chopped
30g flaked almonds
1 tsp vanilla extract,
    homemade (see page
    249) or shop-bought
1 heaped tsp ground
    cinnamon
½ tsp ground ginger
pinch salt
1 tbsp demerara sugar

Preheat the oven to 180°C/160°C fan/350°F/Gas mark 4.

In a medium bowl, combine the blueberries, plums, sugar, cornflour and lemon juice and toss gently until evenly coated. Transfer to a medium-sized roasting dish.

In a medium bowl, combine the flour and butter. Rub in the butter with your fingertips until you have a sandy mixture with a few larger lumps. Use the end of a kitchen knife to stir in the oats, sugar, almonds, vanilla, spices and salt to form a loose, crumbly dough.

Sprinkle the crumble mixture over the fruit without packing it down, followed by the demerara sugar. Bake for 30–35 minutes or until the top is crisp and golden and the fruit is bubbling around the edges. Remove from the oven and allow to cool for 10 minutes before serving.

Homemade hint

Any combination of stone fruits – fresh or frozen – is good here, meaning you can enjoy this crumble all year round. Peach and blackberry or apricot, raspberry and pistachio nuts are both tried-and-tested favourites.

RHUBARB JELLY AND ICE CREAM
WITH CARDAMOM CRUNCH

- - - - - - - - -

Jelly with ice cream was always one of my favourite birthday party treats, so nothing makes my inner child happier than recreating that creamy, wobbly combination. These jellies get their gorgeous colour from forced rhubarb, so seek it out when it's in season.

I like to serve these jellies in individual glasses but if you'd prefer to turn them out, grease the glasses with a little sunflower oil and add one extra leaf of gelatine for guaranteed stability.

Place the rhubarb chunks in an even layer in a large, heavy-bottomed saucepan and cover with the sugar. Pour over 225ml of water and the lemon juice, sprinkle over the orange zest then leave to stand for 15 minutes.

Bring to a gentle simmer then cook without stirring for 10 minutes or until the rhubarb feels soft and tender under the point of a knife. Strain the mixture through a piece of muslin in a sieve set over a bowl, leaving it for about 30 minutes until as much liquid as possible has dripped through. Don't be tempted to squeeze the rhubarb to speed up the process as this will make your jelly cloudy.

Measure the strained juice into a jug (try stirring the leftover rhubarb pulp into yoghurt for breakfast, don't throw it away). You want 500ml, so if necessary top up with filtered water. Rhubarb can vary in sweetness so have a sip – you may need to add a little more sugar, to taste. Aim for a liquid that tastes zingy and that little bit too sweet as the flavour will flatten slightly once chilled.

Place the gelatine sheets in a small bowl of cold water and leave to soak for 5 minutes, or until soft. Return 150ml of the strained rhubarb juice to a clean pan and gently warm. Squeeze as much water as possible out of the gelatine sheets then stir them into the warm liquid, whisking to dissolve. Remove the pan from the heat and whisk in the remaining rhubarb juice. Strain through a fine mesh sieve and divide between four small glasses. Cover with cling film and refrigerate for 4–6 hours until set.

To make the crunch, preheat the oven to 170°C/150°C fan/335°F/Gas mark 3. Line a baking tray with baking parchment.

In a small bowl, mix together the olive oil, maple syrup, vanilla extract, cardamom and salt. Stir in the almonds and oats until completely coated then spread on the tray in an even layer.

Bake for 18–20 minutes, stirring halfway through, until lightly golden. The mixture will look a little wet when you take it out the oven but will crisp up as it cools. Once cool, break apart any clumps with your fingers.

To serve, top each jelly with a scoop of ice cream and sprinkle with the cardamom crunch.

The jellies will keep in the fridge for several days.

Makes 4

For the rhubarb jelly
500g trimmed forced pink rhubarb, cut into 3cm chunks
150g caster sugar, plus extra to taste (optional)
juice of half a lemon
finely grated zest of 1 orange
4 sheets platinum-grade fine leaf gelatine

For the cardamom crunch
2 tsp olive oil
2 tsp maple syrup
¼ tsp vanilla extract, homemade (see page 249) or shop-bought
pinch ground cardamom
pinch salt
3 tbsp flaked almonds
1 heaped tbsp jumbo rolled oats

To serve
4 scoops Vanilla ice cream (see page 149)

Homemade hint

Outdoor-grown rhubarb comes later in the season and also works here, although its flavour is sharper and the colour more of a salmon than a shocking pink. Taste as you go and add a little more sugar, as necessary.

BUTTERSCOTCH DEVIL'S DELIGHT

. . . .

My husband Luke has always had a particular soft spot for butterscotch. More specifically: the powdered butterscotch pudding that you buy in a packet and mix with milk, beloved of many a child of the '80s.

This homemade version of that childhood classic stars dark muscovado sugar, real vanilla and plenty of full-fat cream and milk. A cheeky slug of Scotch stirred in at the end makes this indulgent pudding a little closer to a devil's delight than its angelic namesake, but the flavour is truly divine.

Makes 4

45g butter, cubed
150g dark muscovado
   sugar
¾ tsp flaky sea salt
450ml double cream
3 tbsp cornflour
350ml milk
seeds of half a vanilla
   pod
1–2 tbsp whisky
handful cocoa nibs, to
   serve

In a medium saucepan, brown 30g of the butter (see page 10). Once golden and toasty smelling, stir in the sugar and salt. Remove from the heat and whisk in 150ml of the cream.

In a medium bowl, whisk the cornflour with 50ml of the milk. Whisk in the brown butter mixture followed by the remaining milk. Return everything to the saucepan and bring to a simmer over a medium heat. Cook for 3 minutes, stirring constantly, until thickened.

Remove the pan from the heat then stir in the remaining butter, vanilla seeds and 1 tbsp whisky until smooth. Press cling film onto the top to prevent a skin forming and allow to cool completely at room temperature. Whip the remaining cream, adding 1 tbsp whisky at the start if you'd prefer a slightly boozier pud, then fold two thirds into the cooled pudding.

Divide between four glasses or bowls and chill, along with the remaining cream, for a minimum of 2 hours. Remove the puddings from the fridge, top with an extra dollop of whipped cream and sprinkle of cocoa nibs, then serve.

WHAT'S FOR PUDDING?

BRITISH SUMMER MESS

Whenever we visited my granny's farm in the summer, my mum and brother would head out early to the local 'pick your own' to stock up on British berries. Several industrious hours later, they'd return to find my dad and me still at breakfast, too lazy to help with the picking, but more than happy to eat all the spoils.

Eton mess is a great thing to make when you've got a glut of strawberries. Soaking them in Pimm's adds a subtle sweetness rather than anything overly boozy, but if you're making this for children, you could replace the alcohol with orange juice.

Preheat the oven to 140°C/120°C fan/280°F/Gas mark 2. Line two baking trays with baking parchment.

In a stand mixer fitted with the whisk attachment or in a large, clean, dry bowl using a hand-held electric mixer, whisk the egg whites until thick and foamy. Whisk in the caster sugar, a little at a time, until fully incorporated then whisk for a further 2–3 minutes until the meringue is really thick and glossy.

Sift over half the icing sugar and fold gently to combine, followed by the other half. Spoon or pipe the meringue onto your prepared trays in shallow rounds 6–8cm wide, leaving a couple of centimetres between each. Don't worry too much about how they look – you'll only be smashing them up later.

Turn the oven down to 120°C/100°C fan/250°F/Gas mark ½ and bake the meringues for 1½–2 hours until crisp, lightly golden and the bottoms sound hollow when tapped. Turn off the oven and leave the meringues inside to cool completely without opening the door.

For the strawberries and sauce, combine the chopped strawberries, Pimm's, sugar, mint leaves, lemon juice and orange zest in a medium bowl. Cover then leave to macerate in the fridge for 1 hour. Pick out the mint leaves.

Transfer half the strawberries and all their liquid to a food processor or blender and whizz until smooth. Whip the cream until thick and floppy then fold in the strawberries. Crumble the cooled meringues into the cream, reserving a small handful to garnish.

Divide half the strawberry meringue cream between six glasses then spoon over half of the strawberry sauce. Repeat with a second layer then top with crumbled meringue and the reserved strawberries.

Though it's best eaten straight away, the mess can be prepared up to 1 hour in advance and chilled. The meringues will keep for just under 2 weeks in an airtight container.

GOOSEBERRY OR RHUBARB MESS

Replace the strawberry and Pimm's mixture with stewed gooseberries (see page 132) or leftover rhubarb from making the jellies on page 112.

Serves 6

For the meringue
3 egg whites, at room temperature
100g caster sugar
75g icing sugar

For the strawberries and syrup
600g fresh strawberries, hulled and roughly chopped, reserving 6 whole to garnish
2 tbsp Pimm's
1 tbsp caster sugar
2 small sprigs fresh mint, leaves picked
juice of half a lemon
finely grated zest of half an orange

To finish
450ml double cream

UPSIDE-DOWN LEMON MERINGUE PIE

·····•·····

People are often surprised by how clumsy I am. Barely a week in my kitchen goes by without a minor burn, mishap with a mandoline or something getting squashed.

This recipe is the result of my attempt to salvage a pie crust that got dropped on the floor. With its crisp marshmallowy base and toasty nuggets of almond shortbread, it's an upside-down pie that's all sorts of right.

Preheat the oven to 190°C/170°C fan/375°F/Gas mark 5. Line a baking tray with baking parchment.

In a medium bowl, rub the butter into the flour with your fingertips until the mixture resembles breadcrumbs. Add the sugar, vanilla extract, almonds and salt and mix to form a crumbly dough. Scatter on your prepared tray and use your fingers to press together into popcorn-sized clumps.

Bake for 15 minutes or until lightly golden, stirring gently after 10 minutes to ensure the crumbs cook evenly. Remove from the oven and allow to cool completely.

Turn the oven down to 140°C/120°C fan/280°F/Gas mark 2. Line a large baking tray with baking parchment.

In a large, clean, dry bowl, whisk the egg whites until soft peaks form. Add the sugar, a little at a time, whisking well after each addition until really stiff and glossy. Using a large metal spoon, fold in the sifted cornflour and vinegar until just combined.

Spoon the meringue into a circular mound on your prepared baking tray. Bake for 1 hour 15 minutes until crisp on the outside but still marshmallowy in the middle, then turn off the oven and leave inside to cool completely.

To make the filling, whip the cream to soft peaks then fold in the yoghurt and lemon curd. Spoon onto the cooled meringue, scatter with the raspberries and shortbread crumbs and serve.

This pie is best eaten on the day of making. Unfilled, the meringue will keep in an airtight container for several days.

Serves 8–10

For the shortbread crumbs
60g cold butter, cubed
80g plain white flour
35g caster sugar
½ tsp vanilla extract, homemade (see page 249) or shop-bought
20g flaked almonds
pinch salt

For the meringue
5 large egg whites, at room temperature
250g caster sugar
2 tsp cornflour, sifted
1 tsp white wine vinegar

For the filling
250ml double cream
175g Greek yoghurt
165g Lemon curd (see page 244) or shop-bought lemon curd
125g fresh raspberries

CHEAT'S CRÈME CARAMEL WITH CHAMOMILE AND HONEY

There's something immensely satisfying about the sound of a crème caramel as it plops onto a plate. Unfortunately the caramel in question can be something of a sticking point (quite literally), setting hard in its ramekin or saucepan if you're not careful.

This cheat's version replaces caramel with honey for a fragrant, fuss-free sauce, which I promise won't stick. Use dark honey here for the contrast in colour and its rich, full-bodied flavour.

Preheat the oven to 150°C/130°C fan/300°F/Gas mark 2. Lightly grease the sides of four dariole moulds or ramekins – about 175ml capacity each – with the oil. Spoon 1 tablespoon of honey into the bottom of each mould then place in a deep-sided roasting dish.

In a medium saucepan, gently warm the milk, cream and chamomile flowers or teabags, taking care not to bring the mixture to the boil. Remove from the heat, cover and leave to infuse for 10 minutes.

In a large bowl, gently whisk together the eggs, egg yolks, sugar, vanilla extract and salt until just combined. Try not to incorporate too much air: this will keep the custard creamier.

Remove the chamomile flowers or teabags from the milk, squeezing to extract as much flavour as possible. Gently reheat the milk to just below a simmer then pour over the egg mixture, whisking continuously until combined. Strain the mixture through a fine mesh sieve into a jug, then divide equally between the four moulds.

Pour hand-hot water into the roasting dish, two thirds of the way up the sides of each mould, taking care not to splash the custard. Bake for 40–50 minutes, until the custard has set firm to the touch with a slight wobble and a knife inserted in the middle comes out clean.

Remove from the oven and allow to cool at room temperature. Cover with cling film and chill for a minimum of 6 hours, preferably overnight.

When ready to serve, bring a kettle to the boil, then pour the water into a shallow dish. Remove the custards from the fridge and carefully run a sharp knife round the edge of each one. Dip the bottom of each mould into the just-boiled water for 5–10 seconds, wipe to prevent drips then invert onto a plate. Gently shake to loosen, then remove the moulds and serve each custard in its puddle of honey.

The puddings will keep, un-moulded, in the fridge for 2–3 days.

Makes 4 crème caramels

sunflower oil, for
　greasing
4 tbsp honey
350ml milk
50ml double cream
2 heaped tbsp dried
　chamomile flowers,
　tied in muslin, or 3
　chamomile teabags
2 eggs plus 2 egg yolks
40g caster sugar
½ tsp vanilla extract,
　homemade (see page
　249) or shop-bought
pinch salt

COCONUT BROWN RICE PUDDING

Never one for fancy desserts, my mum often made a simple stovetop rice pudding when my brother and I were small and the image of her stirring a pot at the stove is one ingrained in my memory. This recipe is a nod to that comforting childhood classic.

The combination of brown rice and sugar really makes this dish, giving it a caramel sweetness and nutty texture quite different from the milky nursery fare so many of us grew up on.

Serves 6

200g short-grain brown rice
560ml full-fat coconut milk
80g light muscovado sugar
seeds of 1 vanilla pod
1 cinnamon stick
pinch salt
75g sultanas
2 tbsp unsweetened coconut flakes
2 tbsp shelled pistachio nuts, chopped
seeds from half a pomegranate

Homemade hint

For a more luxurious dish, swirl through 160ml of coconut cream instead of the coconut milk before serving.

In a medium saucepan bring 1 litre of water to the boil. Add the rice, reduce the heat to medium and simmer for 25 minutes. Drain then return the rice to the pan.

Add 400ml of the coconut milk, 650ml water, the sugar, vanilla seeds and pod, cinnamon stick and salt to the rice and stir to combine. Bring to the boil then reduce to a low heat and simmer uncovered, stirring regularly, for 40–50 minutes until the rice is tender and most of the liquid has been absorbed. It will look very wet at first, but don't worry – the liquid will reduce. Add the sultanas, stir, then continue to simmer for a further 5 minutes until creamy. The pudding will thicken as it cools so aim for a consistency that is still ever so slightly loose.

While the rice is cooking, heat a small frying pan over a medium heat and toast the coconut flakes until lightly golden, being careful not to let them burn. Remove from the heat and set aside.

When the rice is ready, remove the vanilla pod and cinnamon stick. Swirl in the remaining coconut milk then divide between six bowls and top with the toasted coconut, pistachios and pomegranate seeds.

This pudding is also delicious chilled and I've been known to eat leftovers for breakfast the next day.

The rice pudding will keep, covered, in the fridge for 3–4 days.

CARAMELISED RICE PUDDING POTS

Some nights, curled up on the sofa, I could happily eat plain rice pudding by the bowlful. On other occasions, when I have guests to impress, its comforting blandness feels that little bit too homely.

This recipe is my attempt to make rice pudding posher. Pudding skin – a must-have for some but, let's face it, distinctly unsexy – is replaced by a brûléed crust and there are sticky pockets of jam hidden beneath the shards of crunchy caramel. Comfort by any other name tastes every bit as sweet.

Makes 4 pots

4 tbsp your favourite jam, homemade (see page 239) or shop-bought
800ml milk
120g short-grain pudding rice
seeds of half a vanilla pod
2 egg yolks
150ml double cream
6 tbsp caster sugar
pinch salt

Spoon a tablespoon of jam each into the bottoms of four ramekins about 175ml in capacity. Preheat the oven to 160°C/140°C fan/320°F/Gas mark 2.

In a medium saucepan, combine the milk, rice, vanilla seeds and pod. Bring to a brisk simmer and cook, stirring regularly to prevent catching, for 15–20 minutes or until the rice is tender and most of the liquid has been absorbed. While the rice is cooking, whisk together the egg yolks, cream, 2 tablespoons of the sugar and the salt.

Remove the rice pan from the heat and remove the vanilla pod. Pour in the cream and egg mixture, stirring continuously until combined. The mixture will look lumpy because of the rice.

Divide evenly between your prepared ramekins, making sure to distribute the rice and liquid equally. Place the ramekins in a roasting dish and pour just-boiled water three quarters of the way up the sides. Bake for 15 minutes or until a delicate skin forms and the custard is almost set. Remove from the oven and allow to cool for 10 minutes. If you want to serve these later, they will keep in the fridge for 2–3 days.

When ready to serve, sprinkle each pot with 1 tablespoon of caster sugar so that the custard is covered in an even layer. Use a blowtorch to caramelise the sugar until golden brown – you could also do this under a very hot grill – then leave to stand for a few minutes before serving.

FIG AND HAZELNUT BREAD AND BUTTER PUDDING

· · · · · · · ·

For someone like me who'd happily eat bread and butter for breakfast, lunch and dessert, this recipe needs little by way of introduction. For those who need more convincing about the merits of a dish that essentially celebrates stale bread, the proof's in the pudding. A pudding consisting of softly-set hazelnut custard, a crisp crust, sticky roast figs and crunchy cocoa nibs. Enough said.

Preheat the oven to 180°C/160°C fan/350°F/Gas mark 4. Spread the hazelnuts in an even layer onto a large baking tray and toast for 8–10 minutes, until fragrant. Remove from the oven and allow to cool briefly. Use a tea towel to rub off the papery skins then coarsely blitz the nuts in a food processor.

In a medium saucepan, gently heat the milk, cream, vanilla seeds and pod and salt. Stir in the nuts then remove from the heat, cover and set aside for 1 hour.

Halve the figs and place, cut side up, in a small ovenproof dish. Dot each one with a cube of butter, drizzle over the honey and brandy and roast for 20 minutes until and the figs are soft and sticky. Transfer the figs to a plate, reserving the roasting juices in the dish.

Strain the hazelnut milk mixture through a fine mesh sieve, pressing down on the nuts to extract as much flavour as possible, then return the liquid to the saucepan and gently re-warm.

In a medium bowl, whisk the egg yolks and caster sugar together until pale and thick. Whisk the warmed hazelnut milk into the egg mixture until combined.

Cut each slice of bread into four triangles. I leave the crusts on for texture, but remove if you want.

Pour a little of the hazelnut custard into the bottom of a roasting dish approximately 20 x 30cm. Dip one bread triangle lightly into the buttery fig juices then place, dipped side up, in the bottom of the dish. Repeat to create rows of overlapping triangles across the length of the dish, then scatter over half the figs and 1 tablespoon of cocoa nibs. Create a second layer of bread, then pour the hazelnut custard over the top.

Scatter over the remaining figs then place a piece of baking parchment on the top of the pudding. Press down gently so that the bread is submerged in liquid, then place a heavy object (such as a saucepan) on top. Leave to stand for 30 minutes.

Reduce the oven temperature to 170°C/150°C fan/335°F/Gas mark 3. Remove the weight and baking parchment from the pudding, scatter over the demerara sugar and the remaining cocoa nibs and bake for 35–40 minutes until the bread on top is crisp and the custard set. Remove from the oven, leave to stand for 10 minutes then serve in bowls with ice cream or custard.

Serves 8–10

150g hazelnuts, skin on
350ml milk
300ml double cream
seeds of half a vanilla
    pod
pinch salt
300g fresh figs
    (about 8), any hard
    stalks removed
50g butter, cubed
1 tbsp honey
1 tbsp brandy or orange
    juice
5 egg yolks
75g caster sugar
8 medium-thick slices
    stale white bread,
    homemade (see page
    234) or shop-bought
2 tbsp cocoa nibs (or
    substitute grated dark
    chocolate)
2 tbsp demerara sugar

STICKY DATE PUDDINGS WITH COCONUT CARAMEL

. . . .

Dried fruit is a wonderful natural source of sugar. At Christmas I can happily eat Medjool dates like sweets, but they're even better blitzed into these classic British puds. Available in little cans, coconut cream is thicker than coconut milk, making the sauce beautifully rich and shiny. If you can't find it, whipping cream is fine as a substitute.

Makes 6 puddings

For the puddings
180g Medjool dates, stoned and roughly chopped
60g butter, softened
90g light muscovado sugar
2 eggs, lightly beaten
1 tbsp golden syrup
1 tsp vanilla extract, homemade (see page 249) or shop-bought
pinch salt
150g plain white flour
¾ tsp baking powder
½ tsp bicarbonate of soda

For the coconut caramel sauce
160ml coconut cream
75g butter
60g light muscovado sugar
25g dark muscovado sugar
generous pinch salt

Preheat the oven to 180°C/160°C fan/350°F/Gas mark 4. Grease six dariole moulds or ramekins – 175–200ml in capacity – with butter and line the bottom of each with baking parchment.

In a small saucepan, combine the dates with 200ml water and bring to the boil. Reduce the heat and simmer for 3–4 minutes until the dates have softened: the mixture may foam up slightly. Remove from the heat, roughly mash the dates with the back of a fork and set aside to cool completely.

In a separate bowl, cream the butter and sugar for 2–3 minutes until light and fluffy. Add the eggs one at a time, beating well after each addition, followed by the golden syrup, vanilla extract and salt. Fold in the cooled date mixture. Sift over the flour, baking powder and bicarbonate of soda and combine until you have a smooth batter.

Divide the mixture evenly between your prepared moulds – they should be about three quarters full – and bake for 20 minutes or until risen and golden with a firm top and slightly squidgy middle.

Meanwhile, make your sauce. In a medium saucepan, gently heat all the sauce ingredients until the butter has melted and the sugars have dissolved. Bring to the boil then reduce the heat and simmer for 4–5 minutes, stirring occasionally, until thick, glossy and slightly reduced.

Remove the puddings from the oven and turn them out of their moulds onto individual plates before smothering in sauce. Serve with a scoop of cold ice cream, pouring cream or custard.

The puddings will keep in an airtight container for 3–4 days.

GOOSEBERRY FOOL

While it's traditionally made with a custard base, I like to lighten my fruit fool with tangy yoghurt and freshly whipped cream. The muscovado sugar and honey add a caramel sweetness but measurements here are just a guideline: depending on how tart your gooseberries are you may need to adjust the amount of sweetener accordingly.

The season is short so if you can't find gooseberries in the shops, replace the purée with sweetened stewed rhubarb for equally delicious results.

Serves 6

1 large handful flaked
    almonds
450g sharp green
    cooking gooseberries,
    topped and tailed
3–4 tbsp light
    muscovado sugar
a few sprigs fresh
    elderflower, tied in
    muslin or a splash
    of elderflower cordial
    (optional)
250ml double cream
1–2 tbsp honey
150ml Greek yoghurt
seeds of half a vanilla
    pod

In a small saucepan toast the almonds over a medium heat for 1–2 minutes until lightly golden. Set aside to cool completely.

In a medium, heavy-bottomed saucepan, combine the gooseberries, sugar, 1 tablespoon of water and the elderflower (if using). Cook over a gentle heat for about 10 minutes or until the berries have burst and become soft and pulpy. Allow to cool completely at room temperature, remove the elderflower sprigs (if using), then mash with the back of a fork to create a chunky purée. Taste – if your gooseberries are especially tart, you may need to add a little more sugar.

Whip the cream until it just begins to thicken. Add the honey – up to 2 tablespoons if you prefer your fool a little sweeter – then whip until soft peaks form. Fold in the yoghurt and vanilla seeds.

Fold one third of the gooseberry purée into the cream. Layer the cream and purée in six small glasses, finishing with the cream. Chill for 1 hour.

Scatter with the toasted flaked almonds and serve immediately.

FOOLISH MESS

Try adding crushed meringue (see page 116) to the mix.

APRICOT, JAM AND AMARETTO TART

Though she is delicate and unassuming in many ways, my mum has big, hot hands. Great for kneading bread, less so for making pastry. At home we've always made pastry that could be pressed straight into the tin and, despite its forgiving nature, it always tastes as crisp and flaky as can be.

Inspired by the Bakewell with feather-light frangipane and sticky jam, this tart is topped with apricots roasted into sweet submission with a splash of amaretto. I've also made it on occasion with peaches and plums which are every bit as delicious.

Serves 8–10

For the pastry
100g butter, softened
50g caster sugar
1 egg yolk
150g plain white or spelt flour
pinch salt

For the apricots and filling
350g fresh apricots (about 6), cut in half and stoned
1–2 tbsp caster sugar
3 tbsp amaretto
4 tbsp jam, homemade (see page 239) or shop-bought

For the frangipane
140g ground almonds
2 tbsp plain white flour
½ tsp baking powder
150g butter, softened
165g caster sugar
2 eggs, lightly beaten
2 tbsp flaked almonds

In a stand mixer fitted with the paddle attachment or using a hand-held electric mixer, cream the butter and sugar together for about 1 minute until just smooth. Add the egg yolk and mix until combined, then add the flour and salt, mixing until the dough just comes together in a ball. If it feels very soft, wrap the dough in cling film and chill for 5 minutes, otherwise press it straight into a deep-sided 23cm round tart tin with a removable base, ensuring the thickness is even throughout. Prick all over with a fork and freeze for 1 hour.

Preheat the oven to 190°C/170°C fan/375°F/Gas mark 5. Place the apricot halves, cut side up, in a small roasting dish. Sprinkle over the sugar, amaretto and 2 tablespoons of water then roast in the oven for about 15 minutes until softened but not completely collapsed. Remove and allow to cool completely.

Take the tart shell out of the freezer and place straight into the oven. Bake for 10 minutes: if it has puffed up slightly, gently push it flat with the back of a spoon then continue baking for a further 12–14 minutes until lightly golden. Remove from the oven and set aside to cool completely.

Once the tart shell and apricots are cool, make the frangipane. Weigh the ground almonds into a bowl then sift over the flour and baking powder. In a large bowl or stand mixer, cream the butter and sugar until light and fluffy. Beat in the eggs a little at a time, adding a teaspoon or two of the flour mixture with each addition to prevent curdling. Once combined, fold in the remaining flour and almond mixture.

Turn the oven temperature down to 180°C/160°C fan/350°F/Gas mark 4. Spread the jam over the bottom of the tart shell then spoon or pipe over the frangipane. Arrange the roasted apricot halves over the top, pressing them gently into the frangipane and reserving the juice. Scatter with the flaked almonds and bake for 50–60 minutes until golden and risen. If the almonds look like they're browning too quickly, loosely cover the tart with aluminium foil.

While the tart is baking, scrape the apricot juices into a small pan. Simmer over a medium heat until slightly thickened and reduced by about half.

Remove the tart from the oven. Using a pastry brush, carefully glaze the tart with the sticky syrup then leave to cool slightly before serving.

The tart will keep in an airtight container for 3–4 days.

VARIATION

For something closer to a traditional Bakewell tart, omit the roasted apricots and simply brush with a little warm, sieved jam to finish.

PEAR AND PECAN TREACLE TART

Adored by sweet-toothed Brits for decades, treacle tart achieved global recognition in the Harry Potter books as their hero's favourite dessert. I think the fact that he chose this simple, syrupy pudding over anything more magical is firm testament to its deliciousness.

Treacle tart should be sweet, gooey and slightly chewy with a flaky crust. I use equal amounts of plain and wholemeal spelt flour in the pastry, but feel free to use all plain white flour if that's what you have to hand.

Serves 8–10

For the pastry
100g butter, softened
1 tbsp caster sugar
1 egg yolk
75g plain white flour
75g wholemeal spelt
  flour
pinch salt

For the filling
115g slightly stale
  brown bread, crusts
  on unless especially
  gnarly, homemade
  (see page 235,
  wholemeal variation)
  or shop-bought
350g golden syrup
1 small pear, skin-on,
  cored
90ml double cream
1 egg yolk
2 tsp lemon juice
pinch salt
100g pecan halves

In a stand mixer fitted with the paddle attachment or using a hand-held electric mixer, cream the butter and sugar together for about 1 minute until just smooth. Add the egg yolk and mix until combined, then add the flours and salt, mixing until the dough just comes together in a ball. If it feels very soft, wrap the dough in cling film and chill for 5 minutes. Use your fingertips to press it straight into a 3–4cm deep, 23cm round tart tin with a removable base, ensuring the thickness is even throughout. Prick all over with a fork and freeze for 1 hour.

Preheat the oven to 190°C/170°C fan/375°F/Gas mark 5. Take the tart shell out of the freezer and bake for 10 minutes: if it has puffed up slightly, gently push it flat with the back of a spoon then continue baking for a further 12–14 minutes until lightly golden. Remove from the oven and set aside to cool completely. Reduce the oven temperature to 170°C/150°C fan/335°F/Gas mark 3.

To make the filling, blitz the bread to fine crumbs in a food processor. In a large saucepan, gently heat the golden syrup. Coarsely grate the pear then stir into the syrup along with the breadcrumbs. Remove from the heat and add the cream, egg yolk, lemon juice and salt, stirring well to combine.

Place the tart shell on a baking tray and pour in the filling. Arrange the pecans over the top then bake for 50–55 minutes until golden round the edges and set in the middle. Remove from the oven and leave to cool completely at room temperature (it will firm up as it cools).

This tart tastes even better 24 hours after baking and it will keep in an airtight container for 2–3 days.

WHAT'S FOR PUDDING?

BOOZY CHOCOLATE PUDDLE PUDDINGS

One of the very best bits about baking has to be licking the utensils. As children, my brother and I used to fight over who would get the chocolate-covered spoon and I still find it hard to resist swiping my finger round a bowl of uncooked batter.

These molten-middled puddings are the grown-up, dinner-party-approved equivalent of licking the bowl: tender cakes breaking open to reveal a puddle of alcohol-enriched chocolate lava. I defy you not to drop your spoon and scoop up the sauce with a finger instead.

Makes 4 puddings

180g dark chocolate,
    broken into pieces
40g butter, softened,
    plus extra for
    greasing
80g caster sugar
2 eggs, lightly beaten
1 tsp vanilla extract,
    homemade (see page
    249) or shop-bought
pinch salt
60g plain white flour
2 tbsp amaretto or other
    liqueur of your choice

Homemade hint

For a booze-free version, omit the amaretto and reduce the flour to 30g. The unbaked batter keeps well in the fridge: add an extra 2–3 minutes to the baking time if baking from cold.

Place a baking tray in the oven and preheat to 200°C/180°C fan/400°F/Gas mark 6. Lightly grease four small dariole moulds or ramekins – about 175ml capacity each – with butter. Cut out four small circles of baking parchment and press one into the bottom of each mould.

Melt the chocolate in a heat-proof bowl suspended over a pan of barely simmering water (make sure that the bowl doesn't touch the water), or in the microwave, melting in short bursts and stirring well between each one to prevent catching or burning. Remove from the heat and set aside to cool slightly.

In a medium bowl, cream the butter and sugar for 2–3 minutes until pale and fluffy. Beat in the eggs, a little at a time, until fully incorporated then add the vanilla and salt.

Sift over the flour and fold to combine. Gently mix in the melted chocolate, followed by the alcohol to make a smooth, thick batter.

Divide the batter evenly between your prepared moulds and give each one a gentle tap on the work surface to level the top. Remove the baking tray from the hot oven and place your puddings on it. Bake for 8–10 minutes until the puddings look slightly domed and feel firm to the touch.

Remove from the oven and turn out onto individual plates, peeling off any baking parchment stuck to the tops. Serve immediately.

CHOCOLATE MOUSSE WITH CAPPUCCINO CREAM

Nothing beats my mum's chocolate mousse. Appearing only on special occasions in our childhood – and enjoyed all the more because of it – her mousse was (and still is) the most chocolaty I've ever tasted, served in tiny ramekins with a squirt of cream from a can (this was the '80s after all). The trick here is to let the chocolate shine: the only dairy in this recipe is the cappuccino cream spooned on top.

Makes 8 espresso cups or 4 ramekins

For the mousse
125g dark chocolate, chopped
2 tbsp strongly-brewed coffee
2 eggs, separated
pinch salt
2 heaped tbsp caster sugar

For the cappuccino cream
125ml double cream
1 tbsp strongly-brewed coffee
1 tbsp caster sugar
½ tsp vanilla extract, homemade (page 249) or shop-bought
1 tbsp cocoa nibs or espresso beans (optional)

To make the mousse, melt the chocolate, coffee and 2 tablespoons of water in a heat-proof bowl suspended over a pan of barely simmering water (make sure that the bowl doesn't touch the water). Remove from the heat and set aside to cool for 2–3 minutes, then stir in the egg yolks until smooth.

In a clean, dry bowl, whisk the egg whites and salt until soft peaks form. Adding a little sugar at a time, continue to whisk until glossy, stiff peaks form.

Using a large metal spoon, gently fold about one quarter of the egg whites into the chocolate mixture to loosen it. Tip in the remaining whipped egg whites and gently fold until combined, taking care not to knock out too much air. The more gently you fold, the lighter the mousse will be.

Divide between eight little espresso cups or four ramekins. Cover with cling film and chill for at least 3 hours.

To make the cappuccino cream, whip the cream, coffee, sugar and vanilla extract until soft peaks form.

To serve, top each mousse with a spoonful of cappuccino cream and sprinkle with cocoa nibs or espresso beans, if using. Serve with the remaining cream on the side.

The mousse will keep in the fridge for up to 3 days.

THE ICE CREAM VAN

MEMORIES
MADE FROM
MELTING
MOMENTS

VANILLA CUSTARD   148

VANILLA ICE CREAM (AND VARIATIONS)   149

MALTED MILK CHOCOLATE
ICE CREAM BALLS   152

CHOCOLATE-COATED ICE CREAM BARS   154

PEANUT BUTTER AND JAM ARCTIC ROLL   156

PEACH MELBA BAKED ALASKA   158

CINNAMON BREADCRUMB ICE CREAM   162

MILK CHOCOLATE SEMIFREDDO   164

BROWN SUGAR CONES   166

GREEK YOGHURT SOFT-SERVE ICE CREAM   168

LEMON SORBET   170

PINEAPPLE AND GINGER ICE LOLLIES   172

MINI MILK LOLLIES WITH
CARDAMOM AND HONEY   173

MIX-INS, MILKSHAKES AND SUNDAES   176

THE ICE CREAM VAN

Many of my childhood summer holidays were spent in Italy. In the sweltering heat, trips to the local gelateria were a daily necessity and it's there that I first got a taste for homemade ice cream.

Back home, tutti frutti was about as close to Italian ice cream as it got, but there were plenty of other frozen treats to fall in love with. Choc ices in their blue and white paper wrappers, sticky Calippos squeezed from cardboard tubes, waves of Wall's Vienetta, and the hidden chocolaty bit at the bottom of a Cornetto. And then there was the ultimate in after-school treats: a 99 Flake from the van in all its swirling, frozen glory.

The best thing about making your own ice cream is that you can recreate those childhood favourites, but using ingredients of the quality you'd find in an artisan ice cream shop. I always have a supply of ice lollies and ice cream bars on standby in the freezer for hot, sunny days and there's nothing I love more than seeing the smiles on peoples' faces when presented with a homemade Arctic roll or baked Alaska on special occasions.

Just a few mouthfuls of messy, melting ice cream are enough to awaken anyone's inner child. So have fun, play around with flavours and fill up your freezer with all sorts of frozen deliciousness.

VANILLA CUSTARD

According to my husband Luke, nothing quite compares to the custard that comes in a tin. The powdered stuff so many of us grew up with tastes different from other custards, not least for its distinct lack of egg.

Rich with egg yolks and cream, homemade custard is a joy. It's comforting, perfect for pouring – hot or cold – over all sorts of puddings and not so much more complicated than opening up a tin. Perhaps more importantly, you can churn it into velvety-smooth ice cream: this recipe forms the backbone of many of the ice creams in this chapter.

Makes about 750ml

350ml double cream
300ml milk
pinch salt
125g caster sugar
seeds of 1 vanilla pod
5 egg yolks

In a medium saucepan, gently warm the cream, milk, salt, 65g of the sugar, vanilla seeds and pod over a low heat until the sugar crystals have completely dissolved. (Take care not to bring the mixture to the boil.) Remove from the heat, cover and leave to infuse for 15 minutes.

In a medium bowl, whisk together the egg yolks and remaining sugar for about 2 minutes until pale and slightly thickened.

Remove the vanilla pod from the milk and cream, making sure to scrape any remaining seeds into the mixture, then gently reheat for a minute or so to just below a simmer. Pour the warmed liquid over the egg yolks, whisking constantly, until combined.

Pour the contents of the bowl back into the saucepan and return to a low heat. Cook, stirring constantly with a heat-proof spatula, for about 8 minutes until smooth, glossy and slightly thicker. Do not allow to boil. When the custard is ready, it should coat the back of the spatula.

Remove the saucepan from the heat and strain the custard through a fine mesh sieve into a clean jug. Serve immediately while warm or leave to cool completely at room temperature, stirring occasionally to prevent a skin forming. Cover then chill for 5 hours or overnight.

VANILLA ICE CREAM
(AND VARIATIONS)

• • • • • • • • •

The frozen alternative to custard, vanilla ice cream is a classic accompaniment that improves almost any pudding. Think of it as a blank canvas from which you can then experiment with all sorts of wonderful flavours. An ice cream machine will help you achieve the very best results, but you can make perfectly delicious ice cream without one.

Churn the chilled custard in an ice cream maker according to the manufacturer's instructions, then transfer to a freezable container and press a piece of parchment over the top. Freeze for a minimum of 3 hours until solid.

If you don't have an ice cream machine, pour your chilled custard into a shallow container with a lid and freeze for 45 minutes. After this time, a few ice crystals will begin to form around the edges. Take the ice cream out of the freezer and use a metal fork to whisk the mixture until smooth, scraping down any frozen edges. Return to the freezer and repeat the process every 30 minutes or so until the ice cream becomes almost too thick to whisk. At this point, beat with a hand-held electric mixer. Smooth the mixture flat, put the lid back on and freeze for a minimum of 3 hours until solid.

Remove your ice cream from the freezer 5–10 minutes before serving to allow it to soften slightly. The ice cream will keep in the freezer for up to 2 weeks.

CHOCOLATE HAZELNUT ICE CREAM

Whisk 125g Milk chocolate hazelnut spread (see page 242) or shop-bought chocolate spread and 1 tablespoon of Frangelico (optional) into the chilled vanilla custard before churning or freezing.

Makes 6–8 generous scoops

1 x quantity Vanilla custard (see opposite), chilled

STRAWBERRY RIPPLE ICE CREAM

Whisk together 125g strawberry jam – homemade (see page 239) or shop-bought – and the juice of half a lemon. When the vanilla ice cream has churned (or if you don't have a machine, before the final beating), dribble some of the jam into a freezable container, spoon over some ice cream then repeat in layers, swirling gently with a spoon to create a rippled effect.

CARAMEL ICE CREAM

Whisk 125g Milk caramel (see page 246) or shop-bought dulce de leche and 1 tablespoon of rum (optional) into the chilled vanilla custard before churning or freezing.

LEMON ICE CREAM

Whisk 125g Lemon curd (see page 244) or shop-bought lemon curd into the chilled vanilla custard before churning or freezing.

MALTED MILK CHOCOLATE ICE CREAM BALLS

At teatime, my maternal grandmother would always offer round the same little pot of chocolates. Powdery, soft and malty in the middle, they were unlike anything I'd tasted anywhere else and inexplicably delicious. It wasn't until I was a teenager that I realised she'd been serving us stale Maltesers ...

With a double hit of malt and a milk chocolate coating, these ice cream mouthfuls are a tribute to those chocolates from my childhood. The malty flavour makes me think of bedtime drinks and is wonderfully nostalgic.

In a small bowl, whisk together the malted milk powder and 2 tablespoons of the milk to make a loose paste. In a medium saucepan, combine the paste, the remaining milk, cream, malt extract, vanilla seeds and pod and salt. Bring to a simmer then remove from the heat, cover and leave to infuse for 15 minutes.

In a medium bowl, whisk together the egg yolks and sugar until pale and slightly thickened.

Remove the vanilla pod from the milk then gently reheat to just below a simmer. Pour the warmed liquid over the egg yolks, whisking constantly, until combined.

Pour the contents of the bowl back into the saucepan and return to a low heat. Cook, stirring constantly with a heat-proof spatula, for about 8 minutes until smooth, glossy and slightly thicker. Do not allow to boil. When the custard is ready, it should coat the back of the spatula.

Remove the saucepan from the heat and strain the custard through a fine mesh sieve into a medium bowl. Leave until cool, stirring occasionally to prevent a skin forming, then cover and transfer to the fridge. Chill for 5 hours or overnight.

Churn or freeze according to the instructions on page 149. Transfer to a freezable container and freeze until firm. Line a tray that will fit comfortably in your freezer with baking parchment and freeze that too.

Once the ice cream is firm, use a melon baller or tablespoon to scoop about 16 small balls of ice cream onto the prepared tray. Return to the freezer for 2–3 hours until frozen solid.

To make the chocolate coating, melt the milk chocolate and oil in a heat-proof bowl suspended over a pan of barely simmering water (make sure that the bowl doesn't touch the water). Remove from the heat and set aside to cool slightly.

Remove your ice cream balls from the freezer. Working quickly, use two forks to dip the balls – one at a time – in the melted chocolate. Turn to coat completely then lift and allow any excess chocolate to drip back into the bowl before placing back on the baking parchment. Return the tray of balls to the freezer for 30 minutes to firm up.

Serve 2–3 ice cream balls per person for pudding or single balls as a snack. The balls will keep in an airtight container in the freezer for a couple of weeks.

Makes about 16 balls

For the ice cream
35g malted milk powder (I use Horlicks)
300ml milk
350ml whipping cream or substitute double cream
3 tbsp liquid malt extract (syrup)
seeds of 1 vanilla pod
pinch salt
5 egg yolks
45g light muscovado sugar

For the chocolate coating
350g milk chocolate, chopped
2 tbsp vegetable or coconut oil

CHOCOLATE-COATED ICE CREAM BARS

Until Magnums were invented in the late 1980s, my mum kept a small supply of choc-ices stashed at the bottom of our freezer. My ritual for eating them involved squishing the end into a chocolaty mess before licking the slightly soggy wrapper clean.

This recipe works as both choc-ices or Magnum-style bars. I think it's well worth investing in some inexpensive silicone moulds for the Magnum look, but they taste just as good either way.

Makes 7–8 bars

1 x quantity Vanilla custard (see page 148), chilled
300g dark chocolate, chopped
2 tbsp vegetable or coconut oil
60g blanched almonds, toasted and roughly chopped (optional)

ALTERNATIVE COMBINATIONS

Chocolate hazelnut ice cream (see page 149) coated with milk chocolate and hazelnuts
Caramel ice cream (see page 151) coated with dark chocolate and peanuts
Strawberry ripple ice cream (see page 150) coated with white chocolate
Lemon ice cream (see page 151) coated with white chocolate

TO MAKE CHOC-ICES

Line a 20cm square cake tin with baking parchment. Churn the custard in an ice cream machine or freeze, following the instructions on page 149. Transfer the ice cream to the prepared tin and freeze until completely hard, preferably overnight.

Remove the ice cream from the tin and slice into 8 bars using a sharp knife. Place on a tray lined with baking parchment and return to the freezer for 3–4 hours.

When the ice cream bars are hard, melt the chocolate and oil in a heat-proof bowl suspended over a pan of barely simmering water (make sure that the bowl doesn't touch the water). Remove from the heat and allow to cool for 10 minutes. While the chocolate is cooling, sift the chopped nuts (if using) through a coarse sieve. Discard any fine powder and stir the chopped nuts into the chocolate.

Line a board that will fit comfortably in your freezer with baking parchment. Remove the ice cream bars from the freezer and dip them, one at a time, into the melted chocolate. Lift out using two forks, allowing any excess chocolate to drip back into the bowl, then place on the prepared board and freeze. After 1 hour, individually wrap each choc-ice in greaseproof paper, then return to the freezer.

TO MAKE MAGNUM-STYLE BARS

Divide your just-churned icecream between 8 silicone moulds, smoothing the top and inserting a wooden stick into each bar. Freeze until hard, then unmould and coat as above. The bars will keep, wrapped, in the freezer for several weeks.

PEANUT BUTTER AND JAM
ARCTIC ROLL

Described in Nigel Slater's autobiography Toast as tasting 'like a frozen carpet', the unashamedly retro Arctic roll is a dessert just begging for a little homemade love and attention. Ice cream surrounded with sponge is a simple concept, so the trick is to use the very best ingredients and serve it straight after rolling so that the cake remains soft and light. Think of this as the best peanut butter and jam sandwich you'll ever eat.

Whisk the peanut butter into the custard, then follow the instructions for freezing in a machine or by hand on page 149. Freeze for 1–2 hours until firm but scoopable.

Scoop balls of ice cream onto a large piece of baking parchment in a line about 20cm long and 5cm in diameter. Fill in any gaps so you have a solid block of ice cream then roll up the parchment to make a tightly packed sausage. Twist the ends tight, wrap in cling film, then freeze while you make the sponge.

Preheat the oven to 200°C/180°C fan/400°F/Gas mark 6. Lightly grease a 20 x 30cm Swiss roll tin with oil and line with baking parchment, making sure it comes up at least 2.5cm above the edge of the rim. Tear off a sheet of aluminium foil double the size of your Swiss roll tin.

In a medium bowl with a hand-held electric mixer or a stand mixer fitted with the whisk attachment, whisk the eggs, sugar and vanilla extract for about 8 minutes until pale, thick and nearly tripled in volume. Sift over half the flour and use a large metal spoon to fold it in, followed by the remaining half and the salt. Scrape the batter into your prepared tin then tap firmly on the work surface to get rid of any air bubbles.

Bake for 10–12 minutes until firm to the touch and a skewer inserted in the middle comes out clean. Remove from the oven and immediately wrap the tin in aluminium foil, making sure it doesn't touch the cake itself and taking care not to burn yourself or let out any heat. This will trap in steam and make the cake easier to roll once cooled. Allow to cool completely.

When ready to serve, lay a piece of baking parchment on the work surface and sprinkle with a little caster sugar. Turn the sponge onto it, peel off the baking parchment and spread the jam over one side. Unwrap your ice cream sausage and place it along the short end of the sponge. Roll up the sponge so the ice cream is completely encased and the join runs along the bottom. Remove the baking parchment and trim the ends with a serrated knife to neaten (chef's perks!). Leave to stand for 5 minutes so the ice cream can soften, then serve in slices.

The Arctic roll is best eaten immediately but will keep in the freezer for several days. Just remember to take it out at least 15 minutes before serving or you'll get that frozen carpet texture.

Serves 8–10

For the ice cream
150g smooth peanut butter, homemade (see page 238) or shop-bought
1 x quantity Vanilla custard (see page 148), chilled

For the sponge
4 eggs
110g caster sugar, plus extra for sprinkling
1 tsp vanilla extract, homemade (see page 249) or shop-bought
95g plain white flour
pinch salt
150g of your favourite jam, homemade (see page 239) or shop-bought
sunflower oil, for greasing

Homemade hint

The peanut butter ice cream in this recipe is amazing served on its own with a blanket of Hot chocolate fudge sauce (see page 247) and Whipped cream (see page 248).

PEACH MELBA BAKED ALASKA

When I was learning to bake as a child, we didn't have lots of fancy kit. Our kitchen scales were the ancient sort where you balance your ingredients with weights, we timed things by the clock, and to this day my parents don't own a hand-held electric mixer. Some tools, however, make life a lot easier and it's well worth investing in an inexpensive blowtorch to make this recipe.

Don't be put off by the lengthy instructions here: each step is fairly simple. And the resulting peachy ice cream surrounded with a cloud of toasted meringue is more than enough reward for all your hard work.

Serves 10–12

For the peaches
and sauce
**500g peaches (4–5
    medium peaches)**
2 tbsp honey
**juice of half a large
    lemon**
200g raspberries
**1–2 tbsp icing sugar,
    sifted, to taste**
**sunflower oil, for
    greasing**

For the ice cream
**1 x quantity Vanilla
    custard (see page
    148), chilled**

For the sponge
4 eggs
**110g caster sugar, plus
    extra for sprinkling**
**1 tsp vanilla extract,
    homemade (see page
    249) or shop-bought**
95g plain white flour
pinch salt
65g raspberries

Cut the peaches in half and remove the stones. Bring 300ml water to a gentle simmer in a large saucepan with the honey and lemon juice. Drop in the peach halves and poach for 2 minutes on each side until soft (longer if the fruit is under-ripe). Remove with a slotted spoon, reserving the poaching liquid, and leave to cool completely. Slip off and discard the skins, then blitz the peach flesh in a blender or food processor to a coarse purée.

Transfer your purée to a bowl and rinse out the blender. Blitz the raspberries with 100ml of the poaching liquid and icing sugar, to taste. Pass through a fine mesh sieve to remove the seeds then transfer to a small jug and chill.

Lightly grease a 1kg loaf tin with sunflower oil then line with cling film. Fold two thirds of the peach purée into the chilled vanilla custard before freezing according to the instructions on page 149. When the ice cream is frozen but still soft, swirl in the remaining peach purée then transfer to the prepared loaf tin. Cover with cling film and freeze for at least 6 hours or until firm.

To make the sponge, preheat the oven to 200°C/180°C fan/400°F/Gas mark 6. Lightly grease a 20 x 30cm Swiss roll tin and line with baking parchment, making sure it comes up at least 2.5cm above the edge of the rim.

In a medium bowl with a hand-held electric mixer or a stand mixer fitted with the whisk attachment, whisk the eggs, sugar and vanilla extract for about 8 minutes until pale, thick and nearly tripled in volume. Sift over half the flour and use a large metal spoon to fold it in, followed by the remaining flour and the salt. Scrape the batter into the prepared tin and dot the raspberries over the top. Bake for 10–12 minutes until firm to the touch and a skewer inserted in the middle comes out clean. Remove from the oven and leave to cool completely in the tin.

Transfer your sponge to a serving board that will fit in your freezer and remove the baking parchment. Remove your ice cream block from the freezer and invert on top of the sponge. Trim the sponge to the same size as the ice cream block and return to the freezer, along with any trimmed sponge pieces (which can be frozen and used another time).

In a large heat-proof bowl suspended over a pan of barely simmering water (make sure that the bowl doesn't touch the water), combine the egg whites and sugar. Heat – stirring occasionally – until the sugar dissolves and the mixture reaches 60°C on a sugar thermometer. If you don't have a sugar thermometer, after 3–4 minutes try rubbing the mixture between your fingers – there should be no graininess from the sugar.

Remove from the heat and transfer to a stand mixer fitted with the whisk attachment. Add the vanilla extract, then whisk on high speed for about 8 minutes until the meringue is thick and glossy and the bowl no longer feels warm to the touch. (It's important that the meringue isn't warm or it will melt your ice cream.)

Remove the ice cream and sponge from the freezer and spoon or pipe meringue over the top and sides until completely covered. Use a blowtorch to toast the meringue then serve immediately with the raspberry sauce.

The baked Alaska will keep in the freezer for 3–4 days. If serving from frozen, take it out to soften about 10 minutes before.

For the meringue
4 egg whites, at room temperature
240g caster sugar
1 tsp vanilla extract, homemade (see page 249) or shop-bought

CINNAMON BREADCRUMB ICE CREAM

Brown bread ice cream is one of the first ice cream recipes I learned to make as a child. Here, caramelised nuggets of breadcrumb snuggle down in brown sugar and cinnamon custard to make a comforting autumnal treat. First crunchy and praline-like, this ice cream develops a softer texture in the freezer not a million miles from cookies and cream.

Start by making the breadcrumbs. Preheat the oven to 180°C/160°C fan/350°F/Gas mark 4 and line a baking tray with baking parchment.

In a small bowl, rub together the bread, sugar and salt to create coarse breadcrumbs, then scatter in an even layer over the tray. Bake for 12–15 minutes until golden and caramelised, then remove from the oven and set aside to cool completely.

In a medium saucepan, gently warm the cream, milk, muscovado sugar, cinnamon sticks and salt for about 3 minutes or until the sugar crystals have completely dissolved. Take care not to bring the mixture to the boil. Remove from the heat, cover and leave to infuse for 30 minutes.

In a medium bowl, whisk together the egg yolks, caster sugar and ground cinnamon until pale and slightly thickened.

Remove the cinnamon sticks from the milk then gently reheat to just below a simmer. Pour the warmed liquid over the egg yolks, whisking constantly until combined.

Pour the contents of the bowl back into the saucepan and return to a low heat. Cook, stirring constantly with a heat-proof spatula, for about 8 minutes until smooth, glossy and slightly thicker. Do not allow to boil. When the custard is ready, it should coat the back of the spatula.

Remove the saucepan from the heat and strain the custard through a fine mesh sieve into a medium bowl. Leave to cool completely at room temperature, stirring occasionally to prevent a skin forming then cover, transfer to the fridge and chill for at least 5 hours or until really cold.

Once chilled, churn the ice cream in a machine according to your manufacturer's instructions or freeze by hand following the instructions on page 149. When frozen but still soft, crumble in the breadcrumbs, fold to combine then transfer to a container and freeze until firm. The ice cream will keep in the freezer for up to 2 weeks.

GINGERBREAD CRUMB ICE CREAM

Replace the caramelised breadcrumbs with the same quantity of Spiced gingerbread (see page 42) crumbled into chunks for a double hit of spice.

Makes 6–8 generous scoops

For the breadcrumbs
100g slightly stale brown bread, homemade (see page 234) or shop-bought
90g light muscovado sugar
generous pinch salt

For the ice cream
350ml double cream
300ml milk
75g light muscovado sugar
4 small cinnamon sticks
pinch salt
5 egg yolks
45g caster sugar
½ tsp ground cinnamon

MINT CHOCOLATE SEMIFREDDO

Growing up in the '80s, it seemed like everyone's mum had a frozen Vienetta on standby for special occasions. With smooth waves of ice cream beneath crunchy chocolate shards, the mint version was always my favourite.

Here, the coconut oil gives the chocolate layers their characteristic crack. A semifreddo base made from softly whipped egg whites, yolks and cream, means you don't need an ice cream machine for this recipe. It contains raw eggs, so try to use ones from a reliable source.

Serves 8–10

- 1 tbsp coconut oil, plus extra for greasing
- 150g dark chocolate, chopped
- 2 tsp peppermint extract
- 3 medium eggs, separated
- pinch salt
- ¼ tsp cream of tartar
- 75g caster sugar
- 240ml double cream
- about 14 Chocolate coconut mint thins, homemade (see page 191) or shop-bought

Homemade hint

Coconut oil is available in most supermarkets, but if you can't find it, grease the tin with sunflower oil and omit the oil from the melted chocolate.

Lightly grease the inside of a 1kg loaf tin with coconut oil and line with cling film. Cut out a piece of baking parchment to fit in the bottom of the tin and place on top of the cling film.

Melt the chocolate, coconut oil and 1 teaspoon of the peppermint extract in a bowl suspended over a pan of simmering water (make sure that the bowl doesn't touch the water) stirring to combine. Remove from the heat and set aside to cool slightly.

In a large, clean, dry bowl, whisk the egg whites and salt until frothy. Add the cream of tartar then continue whisking until medium-stiff peaks form. In a separate large bowl, whisk the egg yolks and sugar until pale and almost doubled in size. In a third bowl (lots of washing up but it's worth it), whip the cream and the remaining teaspoon of peppermint extract to soft peaks.

Fold the egg yolks into the whipped cream, followed carefully by the egg whites, folding gently until you have a streak-free mixture.

Lay the mint thins along the bottom and sides of the prepared tin. Drizzle some of the melted chocolate over the bottom and sides of the tin. Spoon a third of your semifreddo mixture into the tin then drizzle over half of the remaining chocolate. Repeat, finishing with the remaining semifreddo. Smooth the surface flat then place a rectangle of baking parchment on the surface, wrap with cling film and freeze for a minimum of 4 hours.

Slice when very cold, using a heated knife.

The semifreddo will keep, wrapped, in the freezer for 3–4 days.

BROWN SUGAR CONES

. . . .

It makes me a little bit sad when someone finishes an ice cream and chucks away the cone. I'm pretty sure it's the same someone who cuts the crusts off bread, so if that sounds like you please trust me, you're really missing out in both instances.

This simple recipe is adapted from David Lebovitz's brilliant ice cream book, The Perfect Scoop. With a caramel sweetness from muscovado sugar, each crunchy homemade cone is utterly irresistible: I defy anyone not to finish every last bite.

Line two large baking trays with baking parchment and set out a small cone roller (see page 13 for Suppliers). If you don't have a cone roller, you can make one by cutting out a circle of flexible card 15cm in diameter. Roll the card into a cone shape, making the bottom hole as small as possible, then secure with sellotape. Wrap the outside of the cone with aluminium foil.

In a medium bowl, whisk together the egg whites, muscovado sugar, vanilla extract and salt until smooth. Whisk in the melted butter – the mixture will thicken slightly – followed by the sifted flour to form a smooth batter. Leave to rest for 5 minutes.

Preheat the oven to 180°C/160°C fan/350°F/Gas mark 4. Spoon 2 tablespoons of batter onto one side of one of your prepared trays. Use a palette knife to spread the batter into a circle approximately 15cm across. You should be able to fit a second circle of batter on the other side of the tray, leaving a gap between the two.

Bake for 10–15 minutes or until lightly golden. While these cones are baking, spread two more circles of batter on the second tray.

Remove the first tray from the oven and put the second tray in. Immediately use a palette knife to carefully flip both cooked circles over. Working quickly, place your cone roller on one circle with the point about 0.5cm from the edge and tightly wrap the circle round it. Press the seam firmly on the work surface to seal and pinch the bottom of the cone if there's a hole. Slide the cone off the cone form and place on a wire rack to cool and firm up completely. Repeat with the second circle and don't worry if these first two cones look a little bit misshapen. Think of them as a practice run: they'll still taste great.

By the time you've shaped your first two cones, your second tray of circles should be nearly ready. Roll these up, as above, so you have four finished cones, then repeat the process with the remaining batter.

The cones will keep in an airtight container for up to 1 week.

Makes 6–8 cones

3 egg whites
150g light muscovado
** sugar**
1 tsp vanilla extract,
** homemade (see page**
** 249) or shop-bought**
pinch salt
75g butter, melted and
** cooled**
110g plain white flour,
** sifted**

Homemade hint

To make a Cornetto of sorts, dip the outer rim of one cone in 30g chocolate melted with 1 teaspoon butter. Spoon the remaining melted chocolate inside the cone, swirling so it coats the sides then collects in the bottom. Allow to cool completely at room temperature, then fill with ice cream before topping with a little more melted chocolate and a handful of chopped nuts.

GREEK YOGHURT SOFT-SERVE ICE CREAM

Much as I adore Italian gelato and custard-based ice creams, the nostalgic part of my heart will always have a soft spot (pun intended) for ice cream from a van. Swirled into a cone with a crumbling chocolate flake, it's the taste of my childhood and British summertime all rolled into one.

This soft-serve is inspired by those childhood cones, with a tangy Greek yoghurt twist. Egg whites and gelatine might sound like unusual ingredients but combined they give this frozen yoghurt its luscious velvety smoothness. You do need an ice cream machine for this recipe.

Serves 4

1 sheet platinum-grade fine leaf gelatine
3 tbsp honey
2 egg whites, at room temperature
50g caster sugar
500g Greek yoghurt
1 tsp vanilla extract, homemade (see page 249) or shop-bought
milk chocolate flakes, to serve (optional)

Place the gelatine sheet in a bowl of cold water and soak for 5 minutes. In a small saucepan, gently warm the honey then remove from the heat. Squeeze as much water as possible out of the gelatine then add it to the warm honey, stirring to dissolve.

In a stand mixer fitted with the whisk attachment, or in a large clean, dry bowl with a hand-held electric mixer, whisk the egg whites until soft peaks form. In a separate small saucepan, heat the sugar with 3 tablespoons of water, until the sugar has dissolved, then bring to the boil. Boil for 1 minute then remove from the heat.

Start whisking the egg whites again on slow speed. Pour the sugar syrup in a continuous stream into the egg whites. Once incorporated, turn the speed up to high and whisk for about 3 minutes until you have a thick, glossy meringue and the bowl no longer feels warm to the touch.

In a medium bowl, whisk together the Greek yoghurt and vanilla extract. Whisk in the honey and gelatine mixture. Use a metal spoon to fold in one third of the meringue, loosening the mixture slightly. Fold in the remaining meringue until smooth and well incorporated.

Churn immediately in an ice cream machine until just frozen.

To recreate the classic Mr. Whippy swirl, spoon into a piping bag fitted with a large star nozzle and pipe into small glasses or Brown sugar cones (see page 166), topped with a milk chocolate flake, if you like.

This soft-serve is best eaten immediately.

LEMON SORBET

After a big meal, there's nothing more satisfying than a spoonful or two of sweet, palate-cleansing sorbet. Inspired by one of my favourite trattorias in Italy, these hollowed-out lemons are the perfect size. Serving sorbet in this way not only saves on washing up, it adds an extra lemony oomph. Depending on the size of your lemons, you may end up with a little more sorbet than will fit inside. If so, freeze any leftovers in a small container or just eat as you go.

Serves 6

6 medium lemons
175g caster sugar
tiny pinch salt
1 sheet platinum-grade
fine leaf gelatine

Using a sharp knife, cut the top third off each of the lemons: these will be your lids. Scoop the flesh out of each lemon to create a hollow 'bowl', taking care not to puncture the bottom. Pass the flesh and any additional juice through a fine mesh sieve into a measuring jug and chill.

Cut a sliver off the bottom of all 6 lemons: this will help them stand upright. Freeze the lemon bowls and lids for 1 hour.

In a medium saucepan, warm 175ml water with the sugar and salt until the sugar has dissolved. Simmer for 5 minutes until syrupy. Meanwhile, soak the gelatine sheet in a bowl of cold water for 5 minutes. Remove the syrup from the heat, squeeze as much water as possible out of the gelatine sheet and add it to the syrup, stirring to dissolve. Leave to cool completely.

Once the syrup is cool, add 125ml cold water and 175ml of the chilled lemon juice. Taste. If you'd like it zingier, add a little more juice. The flavour will flatten slightly when frozen so your mixture should taste slightly too sharp and sweet.

Strain through a fine mesh sieve to remove any lemon pith, then churn in an ice cream machine. If you don't have a machine, follow the instructions on page 149.

Divide the churned sorbet between your frozen lemon bowls. Carefully replace the lid on each lemon, and freeze until ready to serve.

The sorbet will keep in the freezer for up to 1 week.

PINEAPPLE AND GINGER ICE LOLLIES

Ice lollies are the ultimate summer treat and something my brother and I made a lot as children. We rarely experimented beyond orange or lemon, but there's so much more you can do with different fruits, herbs and spices.

The trick for making the very best lollies is to use a simple syrup base. The sugar improves their texture and you can infuse anything from ginger and chilli to herbs. Try the variations below or experiment with other fruit, adjusting the ratio of syrup to taste, depending on its sweetness.

Makes about 8 lollies

For the ginger sugar syrup
100g caster sugar
7cm piece fresh root ginger, peeled and grated

For the lollies
500g pineapple, peeled and sliced
finely grated zest and juice of 2 limes
100–150ml ginger sugar syrup (see above), to taste

In a small saucepan, combine the sugar with 100ml water. Bring to the boil then reduce the heat and simmer for 1 minute, stirring to make sure the sugar has dissolved completely. Add the ginger, simmer for 30 seconds more then turn off the heat, cover and leave the syrup to infuse as it cools completely. Once cooled, strain through a fine mesh sieve into a small bowl, pressing the ginger with the back of a spoon to extract as much flavour as possible.

To make the lollies, blitz the pineapple in a food processor. Add the lime zest and juice, plus 100ml ginger sugar syrup. Blitz to combine then have a try, adding a little more syrup to taste. The lollies will seem less sweet once frozen, so the liquid should taste just a little bit too sweet.

Divide between ice-lolly moulds and freeze for 20 minutes. Remove from the freezer, insert a wooden lolly stick in each lolly, then freeze until firm. The lollies will keep in the freezer for several weeks.

VARIATIONS

Use the same quantity of the following fruit:
- Fresh strawberries and a small handful of fresh basil leaves, torn
- Fresh kiwi and a small handful of fresh mint leaves, torn
- Fresh mango and 1 red chilli, deseeded and sliced

MINI MILK LOLLIES WITH CARDAMOM AND HONEY

My ice cream choices when visiting a gelateria are utterly predictable: chocolate, stracciatella or, when I can find it, fior di latte ('flower of milk'). Delicate, bright, and cleaner tasting than the more popular 'plain' ice cream – vanilla – it reminds me of the mini milk lollies I had as a child. Here I've added a hint of cardamom and honey to that blank milky canvas.

Combine the milk, cream, honey and cardamom pods in a medium saucepan over a gentle heat. Warm the mixture until you start to see tiny bubbles round the edge of the pan – the beginnings of a simmer – then remove from the heat. Cover and leave to infuse for 45 minutes.

Strain the mixture to remove the cardamom then divide between ice-lolly moulds and freeze for 20 minutes. Remove from the freezer, insert a wooden lolly stick in each lolly, then freeze until firm.

The lollies will keep in the freezer for up to 2 weeks.

Makes about 8 lollies

450ml milk
150ml double cream
4 tbsp honey
8 cardamom pods,
  lightly crushed

MIX-INS,
MILKSHAKES
AND SUNDAES

When it comes to making ice cream, less – as per the Italian approach – is often more. However, more appeals strongly to my inner child and can be incredibly delicious, so here are my suggestions for some indulgent ice cream mix-ins, milkshakes and sundaes.

MIX-INS

Add a crumbled handful of any of the following to just-churned ice cream before freezing:

Wholemeal spelt digestives (see page 21), Oaty dunkers (see page 22), Spiced gingerbread (see page 42), Cardamom crunch (see page 113), Chocolate honeycomb biscuit cake (see page 92), Roasted cherry and white chocolate brownies (see page 98), Chocolate hazelnut kisses (see page 184), Real honeycomb (see page 197), Chocolate coconut mint thins (see page 191), Chocolate peanut butter cups (see page 186).

MILKSHAKES

Allow 2–3 scoops of slightly softened ice cream per person, a generous splash of milk and a small handful of mix-ins (optional, see above). Blitz until smooth in a blender, pour into a glass and top with Whipped cream (see page 248). Add a chopped, frozen banana when blending for extra creaminess, if you like.

SUNDAES

Allow 2–3 scoops of ice cream per person. Layer with gently warmed Milk caramel (see page 246), Hot chocolate fudge sauce (see page 247) or Whipped cream (see page 248), a handful of mix-ins (see above), fresh fruit or toasted nuts and finish with a little more whipped cream.

MIDNIGHT FEASTS

· · · · · · · · · ·

CHOCOLATES AND SWEETS WORTH STAYING UP LATE FOR

· · · · · · · · ·

IRISH CREAM FUDGE 182

CHOCOLATE HAZELNUT KISSES 184

CHOCOLATE PEANUT BUTTER CUPS 186

TEMPERED CHOCOLATE 188

CARAMEL-FILLED CHOCOLATES 189

CHOCOLATE COCONUT
MINT THINS 191

ROSEMARY SEA SALT CARAMELS 192

MILK CHOCOLATE AND HONEY
NOUGAT BARS 194

REAL HONEYCOMB 197

BLACKBERRY AND APPLE PASTILLES 198

ORANGE BLOSSOM TURKISH DELIGHT 200

SHERBET FOUNTAINS WITH
LIQUORICE STICKS 202

PEPPERMINT MARSHMALLOWS 204

Sleeping bags on bumpy floors and crumbs of sugar between the sheets. Torch-lit stories, smothered giggles and desperately trying to keep your eyes open past eleven o'clock. These are the things that midnight feasts were made of.

As an adult, staying awake until midnight isn't quite the task it used to be. Nonetheless there's still something thrilling about chocolates and sweets: indulgences to sneak mid-morning or forage for on an after-dark trip to the kitchen, in your dressing gown, Nigella-style.

Free from artificial colours, flavours and preservatives, homemade chocolates and sweets can be every bit as indulgent and delicious as their packaged counterparts, if not more so. Homemade marshmallows are honestly nothing short of a game-changer, while chewy fruit pastilles, caramel-filled chocolates and peanut butter cups all make wonderful presents for birthdays and Christmas.

If baking is a science, sweet making is even more so. The chemical reactions that take place when working with sugar and chocolate will make you feel part–magician, part–mad professor. For this you'll need the correct equipment, so invest in an accurate sugar thermometer and a heavy-bottomed, deep-sided saucepan and you'll be well equipped to walk the path towards all sorts of nostalgic confection perfection.

IRISH CREAM FUDGE

I remember two distinct types of fudge from my childhood. There were the pieces we got on holidays in Cornwall, individually wrapped in greaseproof paper and packed with enough sugar to make even the sweetest teeth tremble. Then there were the 10p Cadbury's fingers, coated in chocolate and a pocket money treat.

This recipe is a nod to both: creamy, sweet and smooth – not grainy – with a pretty chocolate swirl and barely a background note of booze. Serve in small pieces: this fudge is extremely rich.

**Makes about
40 pieces**

sunflower oil, for
   greasing
450g caster sugar
300ml double cream
125ml Chocolate milk
   (see page 224) or
   shop-bought Irish
   cream liqueur
50ml milk
pinch salt
25g cold butter, cubed
1 tsp vanilla extract,
   homemade (see page
   249) or shop-bought
50g milk chocolate,
   finely chopped
50g white chocolate,
   finely chopped

Grease an 18cm square cake tin with oil and line with baking parchment.

In a heavy-bottomed, deep-sided saucepan, combine the sugar, cream, chocolate milk or liqueur, milk and salt. Heat gently until the sugar has dissolved, then bring to the boil.

Reduce the heat to a brisk simmer and cook, stirring regularly to prevent the mixture catching on the bottom of the pan, until it reaches 114°C on a sugar thermometer. If you don't have a sugar thermometer, you can test to see if the mixture is done by dropping a spoonful into cold water: it should form into a pliable ball that holds its own shape. Be careful if doing this: the mixture will be extremely hot.

Remove the fudge from the heat, stir in the butter and vanilla extract then pour into a large bowl to stop it cooking any further. Leave to cool for 5 minutes.

Using a wooden spoon or rubber spatula, beat the fudge for about 4 minutes until it thickens and starts to look less glossy. Add the chopped milk and white chocolate then swirl to gently combine: you want a ripple effect from the melting chocolate so don't over-mix. Scrape into the prepared tin, spread level and allow to cool completely at room temperature before cutting into cubes.

The fudge will keep in an airtight container for up to 2 weeks.

CHOCOLATE HAZELNUT
KISSES

• • • • • • • • •

Racing along a cobbled street when I was five years old, I tripped and fell flat on my face. After I'd been scooped up and into one of the street-side cafés, a charming waiter presented me with a single, silver-wrapped Baci to make things better ('bacio' being the Italian for kiss).

Wrapped in gold rather than silver foil and beloved of ambassadors' receptions around the world, another Italian chocolate and hazelnut treat is a lot more famous, but I'll always have a special attachment to these little chocolate kisses.

Two hours before you want to make these, pop the chocolate spread in the fridge to firm up.

Preheat the oven to 180°C/160°C fan/350°F/Gas mark 4. Set aside 25 hazelnuts then place the remaining hazelnuts on a baking tray and toast for 8–10 minutes until golden brown. Allow to cool, then blitz in a food processor until coarsely ground. Sift through a metal sieve to get rid of any really powdery bits, then set aside.

Put the cones or wafers in a small freezer bag, bash with a rolling pin to make coarse crumbs and tip into a bowl. Line a tray that will fit in your freezer with baking parchment.

Take the chocolate spread out of the fridge and scoop out a heaped teaspoon (about 15g). Working quickly, roll it into a ball, pressing a single hazelnut into the middle so that it is completely covered. Roll this in the bowl of wafer crumbs then place on the prepared tray. Repeat with all the remaining chocolate spread. If your hands are very hot, the spread might start to melt – if this happens, pop it back in the fridge for a few minutes to firm up again. Freeze the tray of balls for 1 hour, until firm.

Fifteen minutes before you take the chocolate balls out of the freezer, melt the chocolate in a heat-proof bowl suspended over a pan of simmering water (make sure that the bowl doesn't touch the water). Mix in the sieved hazelnuts.

Remove your chocolate balls from the freezer and, using a toothpick, dip one at a time into the melted chocolate, coating completely. Place the coated balls on a tray covered with baking parchment and chill in the fridge to set the chocolate.

The chocolates are delicious served with shots of strong espresso. They will keep in an airtight container in the fridge for up to 1 week.

Makes about 25 kisses

375g Milk chocolate hazelnut spread (see page 242) or shop-bought chocolate spread
100g hazelnuts
100g Brown sugar cones (see page 166) or shop-bought ice cream wafer biscuits
200g milk chocolate, chopped

CHOCOLATE PEANUT BUTTER CUPS

· · · · · · · · ·

It's hard to imagine a time when American candy wasn't available in the UK, but the first time I tried a peanut butter cup was at secondary school when a friend brought some back from a family holiday. Nowadays, chocolate and peanut butter confections are available to buy everywhere, but it's much more fun to make your own. The cocoa nibs add a lovely, subtle crunch, but you can leave them out for a more classically creamy mouthful.

Makes 12 cups

100g smooth peanut butter, homemade (see page 238) or shop-bought
1 tbsp honey
1 tbsp icing sugar, sifted
½ tsp vanilla extract, homemade (see page 249) or shop-bought
pinch salt
1 tbsp cocoa nibs (optional), plus extra for sprinkling
150g dark chocolate, roughly chopped
100g milk chocolate, roughly chopped

Line a 12-hole muffin tin with paper or silicone cupcake cases.

In a small bowl, beat the peanut butter, honey, icing sugar, vanilla extract and salt to combine. Stir in the cocoa nibs (if using). Roll the mixture into 12 equal-sized balls (about 12g each), flatten a little to a diameter slightly smaller than your muffin cases and freeze on a tray lined with baking parchment for 10–15 minutes while you prepare the chocolate.

Melt the chocolates in a heat-proof bowl suspended over a saucepan of barely simmering water (make sure that the bowl doesn't touch the water), or in the microwave, melting in short bursts and stirring well between each one to prevent catching or burning, then remove from the heat and set aside to cool slightly. Alternatively, temper a batch of milk or dark chocolate according to the instructions on page 188.

Spoon 1 teaspoon of melted chocolate into the bottom of each cupcake case, swirling each one gently to ensure the chocolate reaches the edges. Remove the peanut butter discs from the freezer and carefully place one in each cupcake case, on top of the chocolate.

Divide the remaining chocolate between the cases (about 2 teaspoons in each), then tap the tin so that the chocolate settles in an even layer. Sprinkle with cocoa nibs, if using, then leave to cool and harden at room temperature.

The cups will keep in an airtight container in the fridge for a couple of weeks. Chocolate peanut butter cups made with tempered chocolate can be kept out of the fridge.

TEMPERED CHOCOLATE

Tempering is the process that gives chocolate its shiny appearance and snap. If you don't temper your chocolate, the cocoa butter can rise to the surface and 'bloom', giving it a cloudy white coating that's absolutely fine to eat but looks a little more 'homemade'. For everyday treats, I find the process slightly tedious, but I've included instructions in case you are planning to give any of the chocolates in this chapter as presents. You will need a sugar themometer.

300g dark or milk chocolate, chopped

Homemade hint

Use 300g chocolate as a minimum for this process. If a recipe requires less, temper the full 300g then leave any leftovers to harden before using in recipes like brownies, cakes and cookies where the appearance of the chocolate doesn't matter.

In a heat-proof bowl suspended over a pan of barely simmering water (make sure that the bowl doesn't touch the water), melt 200g of the chocolate. Stir until smooth and your sugar thermometer reads 45°C for dark chocolate, 33°C for milk.

Immediately remove the bowl from the heat, add the remaining 100g chocolate and stir to combine. Leave to cool to 27°C. (This is the same temperature for both dark and milk chocolate.)

Once the chocolate reaches 27°C, return the bowl to your pan of simmering water and carefully reheat to 31–32°C for dark chocolate, 30–31°C for milk. Be careful not to exceed this temperature or you will untemper the chocolate and have to start again.

To test whether the chocolate is successfully tempered, dip a clean, dry knife into the bowl. Remove to a plate: the chocolate should set hard and shiny with no streaks within a few minutes.

The chocolate is now ready to use in your recipe. If it becomes too firm or drops below 31°C for dark chocolate or 30°C for milk, gently rewarm it until it reaches the correct temperature.

CARAMEL-FILLED CHOCOLATES

. . . .

Loving someone enough to give them your last Rolo is a sure sign of devotion. Luckily this recipe makes plenty, so you can share your affections a little more freely. I make these using specialist silicone chocolate moulds but you could also use mini cupcake cases. If you do, you'll get fewer – but bigger – chocolates from the batch. These chocolates are pictured overleaf.

Melt the chocolate in a heat-proof bowl suspended over a pan of barely simmering water (make sure that the bowl doesn't touch the water), or temper according to the instructions opposite.

Pour the chocolate into two 15-hole silicone moulds so that it reaches the brim. Tap to remove any air bubbles then invert the moulds over the bowl you melted the chocolate in, allowing any excess to run out. Use a palette knife to scrape the top of the moulds clean, then place in the fridge for 15 minutes to set. If using tempered chocolate, it will set at room temperature.

Once the chocolate has set, spoon or pipe the caramel into the moulds until three quarters full. You may not need it all. Sprinkle each with a flake of sea salt.

Spoon the remaining chocolate over the caramel so that it fills each mould, levelling off any excess with a spatula or palette knife. Place in the fridge for 1 hour to firm up – or leave at room temperature if using tempered chocolate – before popping the chocolates out of the moulds.

The chocolates will keep in an airtight container in the fridge for up to 1 week. Tempered chocolates can be kept at room temperature.

Makes 30 chocolates

300g dark chocolate, chopped
5 tbsp Milk caramel (see page 246) or shop-bought dulce de leche, room temperature
pinch salt

CHOCOLATE COCONUT MINT THINS

Along with dodgy bottles of wine and praline seashells, chocolate mint thins seemed to be the dinner party gift of choice from my parents' friends in the '80s. These are my homemade version. Dipping each frozen square is slightly fiddly, but don't worry if a few snap: the results are still delicious.

Sift the icing sugar into a bowl. Add the milk, coconut oil and peppermint extract then stir to combine. Tip the mixture onto a clean work surface lightly dusted with icing sugar and gently knead for 30 seconds until smooth.

Lay a large piece of cling film on the work surface and dust it lightly with icing sugar. Place the fondant on top and roll out to a rectangle 3–4mm thick. Using a sharp knife, divide into 4cm squares, taking care not to cut through the cling film.

Slide the cling film with its marked-out squares onto a tray then freeze for 1 hour until firm.

To make the coating, melt the chocolate in a heat-proof bowl suspended over a pan of barely simmering water (make sure that the bowl doesn't touch the water). Remove from the heat and set aside to cool for 10 minutes. Alternatively, temper the chocolate according to the instructions on page 188.

Remove the squares from the freezer and run a sharp knife over your pre-marked lines to ensure each square is separate. Cover a tray with baking parchment.

Working quickly, submerge a single mint square in the melted chocolate. Use two forks to lift it out, allowing any excess chocolate to drip back into the bowl. Place on the baking parchment then repeat until all the squares are coated.

Leave to cool and harden at room temperature. Once firm, trim off any excess chocolate with a sharp knife.

The mint thins will keep in an airtight container in the fridge for up to 2 weeks, layered between pieces of baking parchment. Tempered chocolate mint thins can be kept at room temperature.

Makes about 22 squares

For the fondant
185g icing sugar, plus extra for dusting
1 tbsp milk
2 tbsp coconut oil, melted and cooled slightly
1 tsp peppermint extract

For the coating
300g dark chocolate, roughly chopped

ROSEMARY SEA SALT CARAMELS

When I was little I'd hold on to a wobbly tooth for weeks, refusing to let my dad or brother pull it out or create any kind of contraption involving doors and string. Chewy sweets were off-limits, but on one occasion a (wobbly) sweet tooth got the better of me and I lost it to a caramel.

These caramels are buttery and smooth with just enough chew and a hint of rosemary to cut through the sweetness.

Makes about 40 caramels

sunflower oil, for
    greasing
200ml double cream
3 small sprigs fresh
    rosemary, leaves
    picked and coarsely
    chopped
65g butter, cubed
50g light muscovado
    sugar
175g caster sugar
125g golden syrup
1 tsp vanilla extract,
    homemade (see page
    249) or shop-bought
large pinch salt

Homemade hint

Wrapping the caramels in waxed paper helps to preserve their shape.

Lightly grease an 18cm square cake tin with oil and line with baking parchment.

In a medium saucepan, bring the cream just to the boil then turn off the heat. Add the rosemary, cover and leave to infuse for 45 minutes. Strain the cream through a fine mesh sieve, then return the infused cream to the pan. Add the butter and muscovado sugar and cook over a medium heat, stirring to dissolve the sugar. Remove the pan from the heat.

In a large, heavy-bottomed saucepan, combine the caster sugar, golden syrup and 3 tablespoons water. Sweep down the sides of the pan with a dampened pastry brush so there are no sugar crystals round the edge. Heat the mixture until the sugar has dissolved then bring to the boil. Cover with the lid for 1 minute then remove, insert a sugar thermometer and cook, without stirring, until the mixture reaches 149°C. If it looks like the caramel is burning in spots, gently and very carefully swirl the pan.

Whisk the warm cream and butter mixture into your caramel and continue to cook until the mixture reaches 120°C. Remove from the heat and stir in the vanilla extract and sea salt. Pour into the prepared tin and leave to cool completely at room temperature then chill for 1 hour – this will make the caramels easier to cut.

Turn the caramel out of the tin and use a lightly greased knife to cut into pieces. Wrap individually in waxed paper squares.

The caramels will keep in an airtight container for up to 2 weeks.

MILK CHOCOLATE AND HONEY NOUGAT BARS

— • • • • • • • • • —

As a child my brother was fascinated by science and astronomy. For his 7th birthday, my mum painted the ceiling of his bedroom with an exact replica of our galaxy in glow-in-the-dark paint. The effect was spectacular: when you turned out the lights at night, those stars could transport you to another place.

Based on another sort of Milky Way, these fluffy nougat bars are equally out of this world. You'll need a stand mixer and sugar thermometer to achieve the best results, but beyond that this recipe is pretty straightforward.

Makes about 14 bars

For the nougat
sunflower oil, for greasing
2 egg whites
350g caster sugar
1 tbsp golden syrup
100g honey
1 tsp vanilla extract, homemade (see page 249) or shop-bought

For the chocolate coating
400g milk chocolate, chopped

Lightly grease a deep-sided 20cm square cake tin with oil. Line the bottom with cling film and lightly grease that too.

In the bowl of a stand mixer, fitted with the whisk attachment, combine the egg whites and 25g of the caster sugar. Whisk until frothy.

In a large, heavy-bottomed saucepan, combine the remaining sugar, golden syrup and 75ml water. Cook over a low heat until the sugar dissolves, then bring to the boil and heat until the mixture reaches 143°C on a sugar thermometer.

In a separate, small saucepan, heat the honey until it just boils, then add it to the sugar syrup. Bring the whole mixture back up to 143°C. While this is happening, whisk the egg whites until stiff peaks just begin to form.

Remove the hot syrup from the heat and, with the whisk running on slow speed, carefully pour into the egg whites in a continuous stream. Be careful not to pour the syrup onto the whisk attachment or it will stick. Keep the mixer on a medium-slow speed until the syrup is fully incorporated then add the vanilla extract and increase the speed to medium-high. Continue to whisk for 3–4 minutes until stiff, thick and glossy.

Use a lightly oiled spatula to scoop the nougat into your prepared tin. Don't worry if some sticks to the sides of the bowl: making nougat is a sticky business but it will come off

(continued)

with a good soak in hot water later. Spread the nougat level then leave at room temperature for about 4 hours until cool and firm.

To make the bottom layer, melt 150g of the chocolate in a heat-proof bowl suspended over a pan of simmering water (make sure that the bowl doesn't touch the water) or in the microwave, melting in short bursts and stirring well between each one to prevent catching or burning. Remove from the heat and allow to cool for 5 minutes, then pour over the nougat in an even layer. Chill until firm.

Once the chocolate has set, carefully tip your nougat out of the tin and peel off the cling film. Using a sharp, lightly oiled knife, slice in half then carefully cut each half into bars, wiping down the knife after each slice. Place chocolate-coated side down on a tray lined with baking parchment and freeze for 1 hour.

To finish, melt the remaining 250g chocolate, stirring until smooth, or temper according to the instructions on page 188. Allow to cool for 5 minutes then remove the nougat bars from the freezer.

Spoon the melted chocolate over the top and sides of each bar, ensuring they are coated completely. Chill until firm then trim off any excess chocolate.

The bars will keep in an airtight container for at least 1 week.

Homemade hint

Try scattering a handful of chopped almonds or roasted peanuts over the nougat before it sets. Or add a layer of caramel (see page 192 and omit the rosemary), for a homemade take on another sweetshop classic.

REAL HONEYCOMB

Nothing has the power to make me feel like a big kid in the kitchen more than homemade honeycomb. Add bicarbonate of soda to a pan of caramel and a magical alchemy occurs, creating shards of golden sugar that can be eaten as they are or crumbled into ice cream and all manner of other desserts.

Unlike some of the other sweets in this chapter, there's no need to use a thermometer. Grab yourself a pan, pull these basic ingredients from the cupboard and get that Friday feeling!

Line a small baking tray with baking parchment.

In a heavy-bottomed, deep-sided saucepan (you need to allow room for the mixture to bubble up), combine the honey, golden syrup and caster sugar over a low heat, stirring a couple of times until the sugar has dissolved. Turn up the heat, bring to the boil and continue to cook until the mixture turns amber in colour. There's no need to use a thermometer here, but if you want to check, it should read 150°C.

Remove from the heat and add the bicarbonate of soda: the mixture will bubble ferociously. Whisk quickly to combine – about 5 seconds – but don't overdo it or the bubbles will start to collapse in on themselves. Pour onto the prepared tray and leave to set at room temperature.

Once set, bash your honeycomb into bite-sized pieces.

The honeycomb will keep in an airtight container for several days.

Makes about 150g

2 tbsp honey
2 tbsp golden syrup
100g caster sugar
1 heaped tsp
    bicarbonate of soda

Homemade hint

Try crumbling honeycomb through just-churned Vanilla ice cream (see page 149) before freezing. The honeycomb will dissolve into the ice cream overnight, making it beautifully soft and scoopable.

BLACKBERRY AND APPLE PASTILLES

The wonderful thing about making fruit pastilles at home is that you can experiment with flavours that don't exist in the shops. The combination of blackberry and apple is one of my favourites, creating a taste of the British countryside in one sweet, sharp mouthful.

Based on the French pâte de fruit or fruit paste, these homemade pastilles are slightly squashier than their manufactured counterparts. To achieve a little more chew, leave to dry for 24 hours at room temperature before packing and storing or eating.

Makes about 40 pastilles

sunflower oil, for
   greasing
500g fresh blackberries
150ml cloudy apple
   juice
1 medium eating apple,
   skin-on, grated
juice of 1 lemon
20g liquid pectin (I use
   the Certo brand)
2 tbsp liquid glucose
300g caster sugar
100g granulated sugar,
   for coating

Homemade hint

Don't chill the pastilles or the sugar may dissolve and your pastilles will become damp. If the room is particularly humid, they might start to 'sweat' slightly: if this happens, simply re-roll in sugar before serving.

Lightly grease an 18cm square cake tin with oil. Line with cling film then lightly grease that too.

In a large, heavy-bottomed saucepan, combine the blackberries, apple juice, grated apple and half the lemon juice. Cook over a medium heat for 10–15 minutes, stirring occasionally, until the fruit is really soft and the juices run. Push the liquid through a fine mesh sieve, pressing down with the back of a spoon or spatula to extract as much juice as possible. Weigh out 350g.

In a small bowl, whisk together the remaining lemon juice and pectin. Return the blackberry purée to the saucepan, add the glucose and caster sugar and bring to the boil, stirring continuously to prevent catching on the bottom of the pan.

Once bubbling, stir in the pectin mixture and bring the mixture to 113–115°C on a sugar thermometer, stirring frequently to prevent sticking. It should look glossy and feel thick against your spatula.

Scrape into the prepared tin, tap firmly on the work surface to level then allow to cool completely at room temperature for 6 hours or overnight.

Once set, pour the granulated sugar onto a chopping board. Turn the giant fruit pastille out on top and, using a lightly greased knife, cut into cubes. Toss each cube in the sugar then leave to dry at room temperature for at least 1 hour.

The pastilles will keep in an airtight container at room temperature for at least a week.

ORANGE BLOSSOM TURKISH DELIGHT

Despite having nightmares about the white witch in the BBC adaptation of The Lion, the Witch and the Wardrobe *as a child, I always thought the box she offered Edmund with its sugar-coated contents and silver ribbon looked enormously appealing. This recipe recreates that infamous treat with a little twist, replacing rosewater with orange blossom water, honey and delicate strands of saffron.*

Makes 30–40 pieces

sunflower oil, for
    greasing
9 sheets platinum-grade
    fine leaf gelatine
525g caster sugar
juice of 1 large lemon
generous pinch saffron
finely grated zest of
    1 large orange
90g cornflour
1 tbsp honey
1 tbsp orange blossom
    water
30g icing sugar

Lightly grease an 18cm square cake tin with oil. Line with cling film then lightly grease that too.

Place the gelatine sheets in a bowl of cold water and leave to soak for 5 minutes, until soft. In a medium, heavy-bottomed saucepan, combine the caster sugar, 300ml water, lemon juice, saffron and orange zest over a low heat until the sugar has dissolved. Bring to the boil, cook for 2 minutes then remove the syrup from the heat.

In a separate small bowl, stir together 75ml water and 75g of the cornflour until smooth. Squeeze as much water as possible out of the gelatine sheets then add it along with the cornflour mixture to the syrup, whisking until smooth.

Bring the mixture to a simmer then cook over a medium-low heat for 15–20 minutes, stirring continuously with a heat-proof spatula to prevent it catching on the bottom of the pan. The mixture will become really thick and gloopy: it's ready when it starts to pull away from the sides of the pan.

Remove from the heat and stir in the honey and orange blossom water. Scrape into the prepared tin, smooth the surface then leave to set completely at room temperature for 6 hours or overnight.

Once set, sift the remaining 15g cornflour and all the icing sugar over a clean, dry work surface. Turn out the set delight, cut into cubes using a knife lightly greased with vegetable oil then roll each cube in the sugar and cornflour mixture. Leave to dry out at room temperature for 24 hours for the very best texture.

These will keep in an airtight container for up to 2 weeks.

SHERBET FOUNTAINS WITH LIQUORICE STICKS

....

Sherbet fountains were the staple of many a midnight feast in my childhood and I can clearly remember on several occasions tossing and turning – princess and the pea-style – over crumbs of sugar in the bed sheets as I tried to get to sleep.

This recipe is pure nostalgia, combining fizzy sugar and thick liquorice sticks. Liquorice is an acquired taste, so if you're not a fan, replace the anise extract with vanilla or your favourite fruit extract. The perfect retro treat for children and big kids alike.

Makes 24 sticks

For the liquorice
2 tsp sunflower oil, plus extra for greasing
250g black treacle
2 tbsp golden syrup
2 tsp anise extract
pinch salt
225g plain white flour
2 tbsp icing sugar
1 tbsp cornflour

For the sherbet
500g caster sugar
1 tbsp citric acid
1 tbsp bicarbonate of soda
5 drops orange or lemon extract (optional)

Start by making the liquorice. Lightly grease an 18cm square cake tin then line with cling film and grease that too.

In a medium saucepan, combine the sunflower oil, treacle and golden syrup. Gently heat until the mixture becomes slightly more runny, then stir in the anise extract and salt. Sift in the flour then cook, stirring continuously, over a very low heat for 1 minute. Remove from the heat and scrape into the prepared tin, using a spatula to spread flat – it will be pretty sticky. Allow to cool to room temperature, then chill for 1–2 hours.

Sift the icing sugar and cornflour onto a clean, dry chopping board. Remove the liquorice from the fridge and tip it onto the board. Peel off the cling film then use a lightly oiled knife to cut the block in half, then into strips. Roll each strip in the icing sugar and cornflour mixture, then leave to dry at room temperature for 1–2 hours, or preferably overnight.

To make the sherbet, blitz the sugar in a food processor for 2–3 minutes until finely ground. Add the citric acid, bicarbonate of soda and orange or lemon extract (if using) and blitz again to combine. Dip a dry teaspoon into the mix and give it a taste – if you'd like it a little sharper, add another teaspoon of citric acid.

Serve the sherbet in a big bowl with liquorice sticks to dip, or pack into individual paper bags.

The sherbet will keep for several weeks in an airtight container and the liquorice strips will keep for up to 2 weeks.

PEPPERMINT MARSHMALLOWS

* * * * * * * * *

Marshmallows never really excited me until I tried making them at home. The difference between what you can buy in the shops and these bouncy, cloud-like mouthfuls is truly untold. This recipe calls for a thermometer and, if not a stand mixer then certainly a hand-held electric mixer: both are worthwhile investments in the quest to achieve pillows of marshmallow perfection.

Makes 20 large or 30 regular marshmallows

For the marshmallow
sunflower oil, for greasing
6 sheets platinum-grade leaf gelatine
2 egg whites
pinch salt
280g caster sugar
2 tbsp golden syrup
1 tsp vanilla extract, homemade (see page 249) or shop-bought
1 tsp peppermint extract

For the coating
2 tbsp icing sugar
2 tbsp cornflour

Lightly grease an 18cm square cake tin with oil. Line the base with baking parchment then lightly grease that too. Place the sheets of gelatine in a bowl of cold water and leave to soak for 5 minutes, until soft.

In the bowl of a stand mixer, or in a large, clean, dry bowl with a hand-held electric mixer, whisk the egg whites and salt until stiff peaks form.

In a medium saucepan, combine the caster sugar, golden syrup and 125ml water over a low heat until the sugar has dissolved. Bring to the boil and cook without stirring until the mixture reaches 122–125°C on a sugar themometer.

Working quickly, squeeze as much water as possible from the gelatine sheets and add them, along with the vanilla and peppermint extracts, to the sugar syrup, stirring to combine and dissolve the gelatine. With the whisk running on medium speed, pour the hot syrup into the whipped egg whites in a steady stream. Take care not to pour syrup onto the whisk or it could splash up and burn you.

Once incorporated, increase the speed, then continue whisking for 3–4 minutes until the mixture is thick and glossy. Scrape into your prepared tin and allow to set at room temperature for 2–3 hours.

Sift the icing sugar and cornflour over a chopping board. Turn out the set marshmallow and cut into squares, then toss to coat.

The marshmallows will keep in an airtight container for 3–4 days.

DRINKS

SOMETHING
TO PICK YOU
UP OR SEND
YOU TO SLEEP

ROSEMARY LEMONADE   210

FLOWER AND HERB ICE CUBES   212

BLACKCURRANT, BLUEBERRY
AND MINT CORDIAL   213

APEROL SPRITZ   216

PEACH AND MINT ICED TEA   219

SGROPPINO   220

FROZEN MAPLE CAPPUCCINO   222

CHOCOLATE MILK FOR GROWN-UPS   224

HOT CHOCOLATE   226

CARAMELISED WHITE HOT CHOCOLATE   229

DRINKS

At my grandparents' house there was a tiny galley kitchen. On one side was a rusty old toaster, which would pop its contents straight onto the floor (much to the hilarity of all of us grandchildren) and, opposite that, an ancient fridge stocked with what felt like an endless supply of homemade lemon squash.

Mum attempted to limit our consumption of sugary drinks, but we were always allowed Granny's lemon squash, fresh fruit iced tea or cordial. At school or birthday parties there was orange squash, served slightly warm from plastic cups, and at bedtime something milky and comforting, topped with marshmallows and whipped cream once in a very blue moon.

I've interpreted these childhood classics a little more loosely in this chapter, to make them more appealing to an adult palate. I hope you'll agree that alcoholic orange squash is an acceptable improvement, and while caramelised white chocolate wasn't a trend when I was little, if I could travel back in time with a spoonful I'm sure my 6-year-old self would have enthusiastically approved.

Unlike baking and sweet making where ratios are key, the recipes that follow are intended as more of a guideline. Experiment with different fruits and flavours, adjust the sweetness to suit your taste or add a slug of your favourite alcohol for parties and on special occasions.

ROSEMARY LEMONADE

— • • • • • • • • •

My maternal grandmother might not have been much of a baker, but she made a mean lemon squash. Whenever we went to visit, she'd send us home with huge supplies, bottled in various mismatched containers.

Aside from involving a slightly scary amount of sugar, my granny's recipe required resting overnight, something I just can't be bothered with when the brief British summer decides to make an appearance. This lemonade has all the same thirst-quenching qualities and is ready to drink within an hour.

Makes about 1 litre

6 large lemons, plus
   extra, to serve
750ml filtered water
75g caster sugar
3 tbsp honey
3 large sprigs fresh
   rosemary, plus extra,
   to serve
ice cubes

Grate the zest from 3 of the lemons, taking care not to remove any white pith, which could make your lemonade taste bitter. Squeeze the juice from all the lemons, strain out any pips, and chill.

In a medium saucepan, combine 250ml of the water, the sugar, honey, lemon zest and rosemary. Bring to the boil then reduce the heat and simmer for 2–3 minutes until the sugar has dissolved. Remove from the heat, and leave to cool completely at room temperature.

Once the syrup is cool, strain into the chilled lemon juice. Fill a large jug with ice, slices of lemon and a few sprigs of fresh rosemary. Pour in the lemony syrup and top with the remaining 500ml water, or more, to taste. Use 500ml sparkling water, if you prefer.

Leftover syrup can be kept in the fridge for up to 2 weeks.

GINGER AND GRAPEFRUIT

Use the juice and zest of 2 pink grapefruit plus the juice of 2 lemons. Make the sugar syrup as above but replace the rosemary with a 3cm piece of fresh root ginger, peeled and grated. Serve with sliced grapefruit and some freshly sliced ginger.

FLOWER AND HERB ICE CUBES

If you're planning a big party, buying ice in bulk is a sensible option. For smaller gatherings with just a few guests, homemade ice cubes make a lovely addition to any cold drink.

Feel free to experiment with different flowers and herbs depending on the occasion, bearing in mind that herbs and strongly scented flowers like roses will start to flavour the finished drink as the ice begins to melt. Borage, nasturtiums, pansies, rose petals and violas all work well. Good herbs to use include lavender, thyme, rosemary, mint and basil.

Makes 24

filtered water
24 small edible flowers or fresh herb sprigs of your choice

Boil the water then allow to cool completely. This will help to remove any impurities and should prevent the ice cubes from being cloudy. Gently wash the flowers or herbs then use a tea towel to pat them dry.

Fill two 12-hole ice cube trays one quarter full with the water. Place a flower or herb sprig face down in the water and freeze until solid. Top up completely with more water then freeze again until solid. The flower or herb will appear suspended in your ice cube.

BLACKCURRANT, BLUEBERRY AND MINT CORDIAL

Something like 95 per cent of British blackcurrants are used to make the nation's favourite lunchbox drink, so do the remainder justice by making this refreshing alternative at home. Serve topped with sparkling water, or champagne for a twist on kir royale. The mint gives this cordial a slightly medicinal quality, which I rather like. If it's not for you, omit for something a little more straightforwardly sweet.

In a heavy-bottomed saucepan, combine the blackcurrants, blueberries, 300ml water and the sugar over a low heat, stirring until the sugar has dissolved. Turn up the heat slightly and simmer for 5 minutes, stirring occasionally. Add the lemon juice and continue to simmer for 3–4 minutes until syrupy, then remove from the heat. Stir in the mint leaves, if using, cover and allow to cool completely at room temperature.

Once cool, strain the liquid through a fine mesh sieve or piece of muslin into a clean jug. Strain a second time if any bits remain, then pour into a sterilised bottle and chill in the fridge until needed.

To serve, fill glasses with ice and a sprig of mint. Pour over a few centimetres of cordial then dilute with sparkling water or champagne, to taste.

The cordial will keep in the fridge for several weeks.

Makes about 750ml

250g fresh blackcurrants, de-stalked
250g fresh blueberries
275g caster sugar
juice of 1 lemon
3 sprigs fresh mint, leaves picked and roughly cropped (optional)

Homemade hint

Blackcurrants contain a lot of natural pectin so be gentle when cooking them: too high a temperature or too long in the pan and you'll end up with jam rather than cordial.

APEROL SPRITZ

I first had Aperol spritz at a bar in Venice in my early twenties. Served over lots of ice and accompanied by those salty little snacks, cicchetti, *it's the perfect start to a warm summer's evening.*

I like to think of Aperol as orange squash for adults, topped up with sparkling wine to make a sweetly refreshing drink. Unlike some other Italian aperitivi, *Aperol isn't overly bitter, just enough so to balance the orange sweetness.*

Serves 2

ice cubes
2 slices orange, halved
1 slice lemon, halved
60ml Aperol
125ml prosecco, chilled

Fill two thin-lipped tumblers or wine glasses with a generous amount of ice. Add 2 orange slices and half a lemon slice to each.

Pour 30ml Aperol into each glass and top with the chilled prosecco. Gently stir to combine then have a sip, adding a little more Aperol or prosecco to taste.

PEACH AND MINT
ICED TEA

Every summer, on holiday in Italy, my mum would buy white peaches to make iced tea. The mixture would steep in a cool, dark corner of the stone-walled kitchen before she strained it into tall glasses filled with ice: nothing more than water, peaches and tea.

Fruit can vary in sweetness, so I've included some sugar here too. Taste as you go and add more, if necessary, to suit your taste. For a prohibition-style drink, try adding a slug of bourbon to each glass before topping with the tea.

Put the tea leaves (or teabags) in a heatproof jug and pour over 1.2 litres of boiling water. Allow to steep for 3–4 minutes, depending how strong you like your tea. Strain into a medium-sized saucepan.

Add the sugar to the tea and bring to the boil over a high heat. Reduce the heat and simmer until the sugar crystals have dissolved.

Turn off the heat and add the peaches and mint. Cover and leave to cool to room temperature.

Fill a jug with ice, sliced lemon and a sprig or two of mint. Strain the tea into the jug through a fine mesh sieve, pressing down on the peach flesh to extract as much flavour and juice as possible. Chill for a few minutes before serving.

Serves 4

2 tbsp **Earl Grey tea leaves** (or 6 teabags)
2 tbsp **caster sugar**
5 medium **white peaches**, skins intact, roughly chopped
a few sprigs **fresh mint**, leaves picked, plus extra to serve
ice cubes
2 **lemons**, sliced

SGROPPINO

In a small Italian town on the Adriatic coast, there's a restaurant my family has been visiting for over 20 years, Uliassi. What started life as a seaside trattoria is now a two Michelin star establishment, but the owners Mauro and Catia are as charming as ever and still make the best sgroppino I've ever had.

Originally from Venice, sgroppino is like a grown-up version of a slush puppy: part cocktail, part dessert and pure deliciousness.

Serves 6

450g Lemon sorbet, homemade (see page 170) or shop-bought
2½ tbsp whipping cream
1½ tbsp vodka (optional)
275ml prosecco
lemon slices, to decorate (optional)

Homemade hint

Mauro Uliassi's original recipe uses just lemon ice cream and sparkling wine. I use lemon sorbet with a splash of cream and vodka. The extra alcohol is optional but gives this drink a little lift.

Place six champagne flutes in the freezer to chill. Remove the sorbet from the freezer and allow to soften at room temperature for 15 minutes.

In a medium bowl, use a balloon whisk to whisk the sorbet until smooth – you want to loosen rather than aerate it. Whisk in the cream then gently whisk in the vodka (if using) and prosecco. Divide between the chilled champagne flutes, decorate with a slice of lemon (if using) and serve.

FROZEN MAPLE CAPPUCCINO

After almost any restaurant meal, my dad will order a tiny cup of very strong espresso. When I was younger, he'd hand me the dregs into which I'd empty an entire sachet of sugar, stir it into a thick coffee-flavoured paste and spoon it straight into my mouth.

As an adult, I'm still unable to drink coffee without some sort of added sweetness. Here maple syrup does the trick, adding an amber richness to a drink that I think beats any you can buy from your local coffee chain.

Makes 2

200ml milk (coconut
 or almond milk are
 also delicious here),
 chilled
125ml freshly brewed
 strong espresso,
 chilled
about 85ml maple
 syrup, to taste
2 tsp vanilla extract,
 homemade (see page
 249) or shop-bought
pinch salt
375g ice cubes
4 tbsp Whipped cream,
 homemade (see page
 248)
cocoa nibs or espresso
 beans, to decorate
 (optional)

In a blender that can crush ice, blitz the milk, espresso, maple syrup, vanilla extract and salt until combined. Add the ice and blitz again until smooth. Taste and add a little more maple syrup, if necessary.

Divide between two glasses and top with whipped cream. Sprinkle with cocoa nibs or espresso beans, if using, then serve immediately with spoons and straws.

CHOCOLATE MILK FOR GROWN-UPS

Think of the delicious dregs you get at the bottom of a bowl of chocolate cereal, add a little alcohol, and that's what you've got here. Essentially an Irish cream liqueur, this drink can be enjoyed in much the same way: cold over ice, in your favourite warm drink or try it in the recipe for Irish cream fudge on page 182.

Makes about 900ml

750ml milk
200g caster sugar
seeds of 1 vanilla pod
1 tbsp cocoa powder
1 heaped tbsp honey or
   maple syrup
1 tsp instant espresso
   powder
a few drops almond
   extract
pinch salt
250ml single cream
200ml whisky, or more,
   to taste

Homemade hint

If you're in a hurry, replace the milk and sugar with a 397g can of condensed milk and you've got a drink that can be made in minutes.

In a large, heavy-bottomed saucepan, bring the milk, caster sugar, vanilla seeds and pod to a simmer over a medium heat. Stir regularly, to prevent the milk from foaming up or catching on the bottom, until slightly thickened and reduced by about half. Remove from the heat. Weigh your mixture – you should have about 400g condensed milk (if it weighs a lot more, continue cooking for a further 5–10 minutes) – then return to the pan.

In a small bowl, whisk together the cocoa powder, honey or maple syrup, espresso powder, almond extract and salt until smooth. Return the condensed milk to a low heat and whisk in the cocoa mixture followed by the cream until smooth. Remove from the heat and take out the vanilla pod.

Blitz in a food processor or blender for 1 minute until completely smooth. Allow to cool for 5 minutes before blitzing in the whisky. Be careful not to add the whisky when the mixture is too hot as it can cause it to split. Taste, adding a little more whisky if you like.

Pour into a sterilised bottle and chill for at least 1 hour before serving. The mixture will thicken and settle as it cools: shake well before using. Stored in the fridge it will keep for several weeks.

HOT CHOCOLATE

One Christmas Eve, when I was young, I couldn't sleep. After an hour or so of peering out of the window on the off chance of spotting a stray reindeer, I woke up my dad. Together we tiptoed downstairs, past the mince pies and whisky on the landing to make hot chocolate, telling each other stories until I became sleepy.

Hot chocolate will always make me think of childhood Christmases. I'm sure you have memories of your own, whether it's a mug at bedtime, on Bonfire Night or after school. Some people add grated chocolate, but I think that the store-cupboard staples of cocoa and sugar make for the best bedtime drink: a taste of childhood to guarantee the sweetest of dreams.

Serves 2

500ml milk
2 tbsp cocoa powder
3 tbsp caster sugar
2 tsp cornflour
pinch salt
2 tsp vanilla extract, homemade (see page 249) or shop-bought
pinch ground cinnamon (optional)
Marshmallows, homemade (see page 204) or shop-bought, to serve (optional)
Whipped cream (see page 248), to serve (optional)

In a medium saucepan, heat the milk until it just begins to steam. Meanwhile, combine the cocoa powder, sugar, cornflour, and salt, in a mug.

Remove the milk from the heat and pour a little over the powdered ingredients, stirring to create a smooth paste. Scrape this paste back into the saucepan and return the milk to a gentle heat, whisking continuously for about 1 minute until the sugar has dissolved completely. Bring to the boil then reduce to a simmer and cook for 3–4 minutes, whisking constantly, until thick and glossy.

Remove from the heat and whisk in the vanilla and cinnamon, if using. Divide between two mugs and serve immediately. Top with marshmallows or whipped cream, if you like.

CARAMELISED WHITE HOT CHOCOLATE

Maybe it's because my husband bears more than a passing resemblance to a grown-up version of the Milkybar Kid, but I have a soft spot for white chocolate. It isn't for everyone, but if any recipe can convert people to the light side, I'd put my money on this one.

When roasted at a low temperature, the sugar and cocoa butter that give white chocolate its almost soapy sweetness caramelise into a dulce de leche-like liquid. Melted into hot milk and cream it becomes a luxurious yet comforting dessert of a drink with notes of nutty butterscotch.

Serves 4

200g white chocolate, roughly chopped
750ml milk
100ml single cream
1 tsp vanilla extract, homemade (see page 249) or shop-bought
½ tsp ground cinnamon
pinch salt
Marshmallows, homemade (see page 204) or shop-bought, to serve (optional)

Homemade hint

If you only want one or two servings, transfer the remaining caramelised chocolate to a clean glass jar. It will solidify once cool but can easily be melted again directly into warm milk.

Begin by caramelising the chocolate. Preheat the oven to 130°C/110°C fan/250°F/Gas mark ½. Scatter the chocolate in a small, rimmed baking dish and roast for 40–60 minutes, stirring every 5–10 minutes with a clean, dry spatula.

At first it will look like nothing is happening; then the chocolate may appear crumbly. Trust the process and as you continue to heat and stir, the chocolate will start to melt and caramelise, turning to a runny peanut-butter consistency and colour. When the chocolate is golden and feels smooth and spreadable, remove from the oven.

In a medium pan, bring the milk and cream to a simmer. Scrape in the caramelised white chocolate and whisk until combined, then whisk in the vanilla extract and cinnamon. Add salt, to taste – a few crystals really lift the flavour – then divide between four mugs and top with marshmallows, if you like.

LITTLE LOAF BASICS

• • • • • • • •

BREAD, SPREADS AND EXTRAS

• • • • • • • •

A LITTLE LOAF   234

PEANUT BUTTER   238

STRAWBERRY, PLUM AND VANILLA JAM   239

MILK CHOCOLATE HAZELNUT SPREAD   242

LEMON CURD   244

MILK CARAMEL   246

HOT CHOCOLATE FUDGE SAUCE   247

WHIPPED CREAM   248

VANILLA EXTRACT   249

Growing up, making bread wasn't something my family did with any particular skill, but I can still remember the excited anticipation as we waited for a loaf to bake. Just as the kitchen began to smell more delicious than we could stand, the bread would be ready. Fresh out of the oven we'd fall on it with glee, slathering salty butter into round after round of still-warm slices and disregarding everything the experts say about leaving a loaf to cool before cutting into it.

Homemade bread is one of life's greatest pleasures. I started the Little Loaf blog as a way of documenting my journey in learning to bake real bread at home, so it feels fitting to open this final chapter by encouraging you to do the same. Hot buttered bread is hard to beat, but for when you want something more exciting, I've included a handful of my favourite spreads too. These can be used in all manner of recipes and, along with basics such as Whipped cream and Hot chocolate fudge sauce, are absolute essentials in 'the Little Loaf' kitchen.

A LITTLE LOAF

Made with milk, honey and butter, this bread is delicately soft with a hint of sweetness, making it perfect for using in desserts. If a freshly baked loaf turns any meal into a celebration, a stale one can end it in style. Slice, toast and serve with any of the spreads in this chapter then use stale bread in all manner of treats from Fig and hazelnut bread and butter pudding (see page 128) to Pear and pecan treacle tart (see page 138) and Cinnamon breadcrumb ice cream (see page 162).

Makes one 1kg loaf

250–260ml milk
1 tsp honey
25g cold butter, cubed, plus extra for greasing
400g strong white bread flour, plus extra for dusting
7g fast-action yeast
7g salt
sunflower oil, for greasing

In a small saucepan, gently warm 200ml of the milk with the honey until the honey has dissolved. Take the pan off the heat. Place the butter and flour in a large mixing bowl and use your fingertips to lightly rub the butter into the flour until you can no longer feel any lumps. Add the yeast to one side of the bowl and the salt to the other.

Pour the lukewarm milk into the flour and mix together using a plastic dough scraper or your fingers. Slowly add the remaining milk, a little at a time, to form a sticky, but not soggy, dough. You may not need it all.

Scrape the dough onto a clean work surface and knead for 8–10 minutes until soft and smooth. At first it will feel impossibly wet and sticky – have faith and try not to add extra flour as this will dry out the dough. After several minutes of kneading, you'll start to achieve the silky texture you're looking for.

Shape the dough into a round and place in a bowl greased lightly with sunflower oil. Cover with a tea towel and leave to rise until doubled in size. This should take about 1 hour: if your kitchen is cold it could take up to 3 hours.

Grease a 1kg loaf tin with butter. Tip the risen dough onto a lightly floured work surface and shape into a ball. Stretch and flatten the ball into an oval disc the same length as your tin. Fold the outside edges of the oval into the middle to form an oblong, pressing down firmly where they join. Transfer your dough to the tin, tucking the ends under slightly and making sure the join is underneath.

Cover with a tea towel and leave for a further hour, or until the dough has almost doubled in size again. Preheat the oven to 240°C/220°C fan/460°F/Gas mark 8.

Dust the risen loaf with flour and slash the top with a sharp knife. Bake for 10 minutes then turn the oven down to 220°C/200°C fan/425°F/Gas mark 7 and bake for 15–20 minutes more. To check if it's ready, tip the loaf out of its tin and tap the base – it should sound hollow. Remove from the oven and leave to cool completely on a wire rack out of the tin.

The loaf will keep for 3–4 days. After that your bread will be stale, but don't throw it away – there are lots of lovely recipes you can make with stale bread in this book.

LITTLE WHOLEMEAL LOAF

Make a wholemeal loaf using the directions above but with the following alterations:

- Replace the strong white bread flour with 325g strong wholemeal bread flour and 75g malted wheat flour.

- Omit the butter and honey.

- Replace the milk with 270ml lukewarm water mixed with 25ml olive oil.

PEANUT BUTTER

Peanut butter sticks to the roof of your mouth like nobody's business, but that's all part of the pleasure. My dad likes to mix it with Marmite – which might well make you shudder – sandwiched together with jam on soft white bread is a more tried and tested treat.

If you're particular about your peanut butter, making it at home is a must. Tweak this recipe to suit your personal preferences, keeping it crunchy or smooth, salty or a little bit sweet.

Makes about 350g

**350g shelled peanuts
2 tsp groundnut or
 other vegetable oil
generous pinch salt
1 tbsp honey (optional)**

Preheat the oven to 180°C/160°C fan/350°F/Gas mark 4. Line a baking tray with baking parchment, spread the peanuts on it in an even layer and toast in the oven for 15 minutes or until golden. Remove from the oven and allow to cool completely on the tray.

Put the toasted nuts in a food processor and pulse for 1–2 minutes to form a fine powder. Add the oil and salt, then process continuously until creamy, stopping occasionally to scrape down the sides with a spatula. Don't panic when the mixture looks dry and crumbly at first, as you continue to process it the nut oils will be released and it will become smooth. My processor takes between 5 and 7 minutes to achieve a really creamy texture.

Add the honey, if using, and blitz to combine. Add a little more salt, to taste, or oil if you prefer a looser consistency, then transfer to a sterilised jar with a lid.

The peanut butter will keep in a cool, dry place for several weeks.

CRUNCHY PEANUT BUTTER

For crunchy peanut butter, keep back 50g peanuts, then pulse into the smooth nut butter until just incorporated.

OTHER NUT BUTTERS

Hazelnuts, cashews and almonds also work here but will need a little less time toasting in the oven.

STRAWBERRY, PLUM AND VANILLA JAM

The first time I made jam was on holiday in France. We spent all morning picking strawberries and all afternoon cooking them before funnelling the fruity red lava into jar after jar.

Nowadays I prefer to make my jam in small batches. There isn't space in our flat to store it in any great quantity and a single jar lasts the two of us a couple of weeks. If you'd prefer to make more, the quantities below can be scaled up.

If you don't have a sugar thermometer, place a small plate in the freezer. In a large, heavy-bottomed saucepan, combine the strawberries, plums, sugar and lemon juice. Stir to combine then leave for 15 minutes until the fruit starts to release its juices.

Gently heat until the sugar has dissolved, then bring to the boil. Add the salt then reduce the heat to a brisk simmer. Stir regularly to prevent the fruit catching on the bottom of the pan until the fruit breaks down and the mixture becomes thicker and more syrupy. This can take anywhere between 15 and 30 minutes.

At this point, start checking the jam for a set. If you have a sugar thermometer, the temperature should read 104°C. If you don't, take the pan off the heat and remove your plate from the freezer. Add a blob of jam to the plate and return to the fridge for 3 minutes. When the time is up, gently press your finger against the jam – if the surface wrinkles, it's ready; if not, return the pan to the heat and cook for a further 2–3 minutes before testing again.

When the jam is ready, remove the pan from the heat, stir in the vanilla seeds then pour into a large sterilised glass jar. Cool completely at room temperature, before screwing on the lid and chilling. The jam will keep, unopened, for several months. Once opened, use within 1 week.

RASPBERRY AND PEACH JAM

Try any combination of stone fruit and berries using the same weights listed above: raspberry and peach is one of my favourites.

Makes about 380g

200g ripe strawberries, hulled and quartered
265g plums (about 3 or 4), skin on, halved, stoned and roughly chopped
200g granulated sugar
juice of half a lemon
pinch salt
seeds of half a vanilla pod

MILK CHOCOLATE
HAZELNUT SPREAD

Until the age of about ten, I thought that Nutella was only available abroad — something my parents would buy for my brother and me on summer holidays in Italy. Seeing it as an exotic, European treat somehow made it so much more exciting than if we'd been allowed it every day.

Full of toasty roasted hazelnuts and rich milk chocolate, this homemade version is every bit as magical. It's delicious on toast, spooned straight from the jar or used in a number of treats that appear in this book, such as the Chocolate hazelnut kisses (see page 184).

Makes about 380g

150g hazelnuts, skin on
**125g milk chocolate,
    roughly chopped**
**1 tsp groundnut or other
    vegetable oil**
50g icing sugar
1½ tbsp cocoa powder
**1 tsp vanilla extract,
    homemade (see page
    249) or shop-bought**
pinch salt

Preheat the oven to 180°C/160°C fan/350°F/Gas mark 4. Line a tray with baking parchment, spread the hazelnuts in an even layer and toast for 8–10 minutes or until the nuts are fragrant and their skins look loose and papery. Remove from the oven and allow to cool completely on the tray.

While the nuts are roasting, melt the chocolate in a heat-proof bowl suspended over a pan of barely simmering water (make sure that the bowl doesn't touch the water) or in the microwave, melting in short bursts and stirring well between each one to prevent catching or burning. Remove from the heat and set aside to cool for 5 minutes.

Rub the hazelnuts vigorously in a tea towel to remove their papery skins. Try to remove as much as you can as the skins have a slightly bitter taste.

Blitz the hazelnuts for 2–3 minutes in a food processor until smooth. At first the mixture will be thick, but as the natural oils release it will become slightly more paste-like. Add the oil and blitz for another 2–3 minutes until the mixture looks relatively smooth.

Add the sugar, cocoa powder, vanilla extract, cooled melted chocolate and salt and blitz for 3–4 minutes more until completely smooth, occasionally scraping down the sides with a spatula if necessary.

Scrape the spread into a sterilised jar with a lid. The spread will keep in a cool, dry place for several weeks.

LEMON CURD

· · · · · · · · ·

While I almost always opt for chocolate over fruity desserts, one spoonful of my mum's lemon curd is always enough to make me realise I could never choose definitively between the two. I make mine as you would custard, tempering the eggs before thickening the mixture over a gentle heat to limit the risk of scrambling. This curd is sharp, sweet and beautifully smooth; if you could bottle sunshine, it would taste like this.

Makes about 350g

**finely grated zest of
  1 lemon
125ml lemon juice (from
  2–3 lemons)
110g caster sugar
2 eggs plus 2 egg yolks
pinch salt
75g butter, cubed**

In a medium saucepan, combine the lemon zest, juice and 75g of the sugar. Heat gently until the sugar has completely dissolved.

Meanwhile, in a medium bowl, vigorously whisk together the eggs, egg yolks, remaining 35g of sugar and salt for 1 minute.

Pour the warm lemon juice over the eggs, whisking constantly to combine then return the whole mixture to the saucepan. Cook over a gentle heat for 2–3 minutes, stirring constantly with a heat-proof spatula, until thickened slightly. Stir in the butter and continue to cook for 1–2 minutes, stirring constantly, until the butter has melted and the mixture is thick and glossy.

Strain the lemon curd through a fine mesh sieve then transfer to a sterilised jar. Leave to cool completely at room temperature then screw on a lid and chill.

The curd will keep in the fridge, unopened, for up to 1 month. Once opened, eat within 1 week.

GRAPEFRUIT, LIME OR ORANGE CURD

You can replace the lemons in this recipe with grapefruit, lime or orange. Just make sure to always include a little lemon juice for sharpness and adjust the sugar quantities to your taste.

MILK CARAMEL

———————————

● ● ● ● ● ● ● ●

I first discovered milk caramel made from scratch in the form of manjar (better known as dulce de leche) whilst travelling in South America as a teenager. Until then, my only experience of the stuff was from boiling cans of condensed milk in a saucepan and hoping against all odds that they wouldn't explode all over the ceiling.

This stovetop version is not at all alarming and tastes utterly divine. I love the Mexican variation, cajeta, made with goat's milk – its slight farmyard aroma works wonderfully to balance the caramel sweetness. If goat's milk isn't for you, cow's milk works just as well.

Makes about 300ml

1 litre milk, goat's or cow's
225g caster sugar
1 heaped tbsp golden syrup
seeds of 1 vanilla pod
¼ tsp bicarbonate soda
large pinch salt

Homemade hint
The longer you cook the caramel, the thicker it will be.

In a deep-sided, heavy-bottomed saucepan, combine the milk, sugar, golden syrup, vanilla seeds and pod, bicarbonate of soda and salt and bring to the boil. The milk will froth up as it boils, especially if you're using goat's milk, so stir it occasionally with a heat-proof spatula or wooden spoon.

Reduce the heat slightly to a brisk simmer. Continue to cook, stirring frequently, until the mixture begins to thicken and turn a light brown. If it catches on the bottom, you may need to reduce the heat slightly. The process can take anything between 15–30 minutes.

Once the mixture starts to thicken, reduce the heat to a low simmer. Continue to cook for about 20 minutes, stirring continuously, until it has the consistency of thick caramel sauce and is the colour of milky tea. You should be able to draw a line through the mixture with your spatula.

Remove the pan from the heat, remove the vanilla pod using your spatula (the mixture will be hot!), then pour into a large sterilised jar. Leave to cool completely at room temperature, then use straight away or screw a lid on the jar and store in the fridge.

The caramel will keep in the fridge for up to 1 month, and up to 1 week once opened. Re-warm in a small saucepan over a gentle heat, adding water or milk a teaspoon at a time to achieve the consistency that you want.

HOT CHOCOLATE
FUDGE SAUCE

. . . .

When I was young I spent the majority of my pocket money on a pony book series called The Saddle Club. *Set in Virginia, it featured three horse-mad friends who would meet regularly at their local ice cream parlour, Tastee Delight.*

When I wasn't wishing my parents would buy me a pony, I longed for American ice-cream sundaes. This fudge sauce is what I imagine they ate – rich, indulgent and entirely over the top in the best possible way.

In a medium heavy-bottomed saucepan, combine the cream, muscovado sugar, butter, golden syrup and cocoa powder over a gentle heat, stirring to combine. Once the butter has melted and the sugar dissolved, bring to the boil then immediately remove from the heat.

Add the chocolate and salt, stirring until smooth. Allow to stand for a couple of minutes before serving.

The sauce will keep in the fridge for up to 2 weeks. Chilled, the sauce will become thick and almost ganache-like – you can re-warm it in a small saucepan over a gentle heat.

CHOCOLATE PEANUT BUTTER SAUCE

Add 85g smooth peanut butter – homemade (see page 238) or shop-bought – into the sauce along with the chopped chocolate, stirring until smooth.

Makes about 500ml

250ml double cream
100g light muscovado sugar
50g butter, cubed
1 tbsp golden syrup
1 tbsp cocoa powder
100g dark chocolate, coarsely chopped
pinch salt

WHIPPED CREAM

Squirting cream from a can directly into your mouth is the ultimate childhood pleasure. In fact, I'd happily still do that now if it wasn't for the fact that homemade whipped cream is so much more delicious. I can't think of many desserts that aren't improved by a generous dollop.

Makes 500ml

250ml double cream, chilled
2–3 tsp caster sugar or maple syrup (or more, to taste)
seeds of half a vanilla pod

Homemade hint

If you over-whip the cream, don't panic. Gently fold an additional 50ml cold double cream into the bowl to loosen.

If it's a hot day and you have room, pop the bowl in which you're planning to whip the cream in the fridge to chill for an hour before you begin. Otherwise, starting with very cold cream is fine.

If whipping by hand, pour the cream into the chilled bowl and whisk vigorously for 2–3 minutes, until it starts to thicken. Add the caster sugar or maple syrup and vanilla seeds, then whip for a further 1–2 minutes until you have delicately soft peaks.

If using a hand-held electric mixer, pay close attention as the cream will thicken very quickly. Once very soft peaks form, add the sugar or maple syrup, and the vanilla seeds, then whisk for another minute or so, until soft peaks return.

Cream can be whipped up to 3 hours before serving and stored in the fridge, but is best served fresh.

VANILLA EXTRACT

When I was learning to bake as a child, vanilla pods were deemed exotic and expensive so we always used extract. Nowadays, you can buy all sorts of lovely powders and pastes, but I love how this homemade version recycles old vanilla pods. All you need here are clean, scraped pods (so not ones that have been steeped in milk), alcohol and patience: a good vanilla extract is at least six weeks in the making.

In a sterilised jar or bottle with a lid, combine the vodka and vanilla pods. Used vanilla pods with the seeds scraped are fine, but if you want to amp up the flavour, start with brand new pods, split open but seeds still inside. Put the lid on, shake gently and store in a cool, dark place (the cupboard is perfect) for 6 weeks, shaking once or twice each week, or until the liquid looks darker and smells pungently of vanilla.

When ready to use, you can strain the liquid and return it to the bottle, if you like. Otherwise leave the bottle as it is, using the extract and adding extra vanilla pods every time you use them for another recipe. For every 3 additional used pods, add an extra 30ml alcohol.

The extract will keep pretty much forever in a sterile, sealed container.

Makes 250ml

250ml vodka
4 vanilla pods

INDEX

almonds, flaked
  apricot, jam and amaretto tart
    134–5
  blueberry, almond and plum
    crumble 110
  gooseberry fool 132
  rhubarb jelly and ice cream
    with cardamom crunch 113
  upside-down lemon meringue
    pie 119
almonds, ground
  almond, honey and cinnamon
    fig rolls 28
  apricot, jam and amaretto tart
    134–5
  coconut marzipan 104
  Jaffa orange cakes 33
  nectarine upside-down cake 81
  spiced strawberry layer cake 83
almonds, whole
  blueberry, almond and plum
    crumble 110
  nut butter 238
amaretto
  apricot, jam and amaretto tart
    134–5
  chocolate puddle puddings 141
Aperol spritz 216
apples
  almond, honey and cinnamon
    fig rolls 28
  blackberry and apple pastilles
    198
  pecan caramel apples 56
apricots, dried
  apricot, peanut and sesame
    flapjacks 54
  pistachio and lime loaf with
    honey and apricot drizzle 84
apricots, fresh
  apricot, jam and amaretto tart
    134–5
bananas
  banoffee pecan éclairs 64–5

chocolate-freckled banana
  bread 105
black treacle
  sherbet fountains with
    liquorice sticks 202
  spiced gingerbread 42
blackberries
  blackberry and apple pastilles
    198
  blackberry and hazelnut
    meringue sandwiches 48
blackcurrants
  blackcurrant, blueberry and
    mint cordial 213
blueberries
  blackcurrant, blueberry and
    mint cordial 213
  blueberry, almond and plum
    crumble 110
bourbon: bourbon biscuits 36
brandy
  fig and hazelnut bread and
    butter pudding 129
bread, brown
  cinnamon breadcrumb ice
    cream 163
  little wholemeal loaf 234–5
  pear and pecan treacle tart
    138
bread, white
  a little loaf 234–5
  fig and hazelnut bread and
    butter pudding 129
brown sugar cones 166
  chocolate hazelnut kisses 184
butter, brown (beurre noisette) 10
  brown butter chocolate-chunk
    cookies 38
  Jaffa orange cakes 33
  nutty, buttery crisp rice squares
    91
buttermilk
  oat and buttermilk scones 50

caramel
  milk caramel 246
  pecan caramel apples/pears 56
  rosemary sea salt caramels 192
  tea and biscuit slice 41
carrots: mini carrot cakes 78
cashew nut butter 238
chamomile flowers
  cheat's crème caramel with
    chamomile and honey 120
cherries
  roasted cherry and white
    chocolate brownies 98–9
chillies, red
  mango and chilli ice lollies 172
chocolate buttons
  triple chocolate caterpillar cake
    86–9
chocolate, dark
  brown butter chocolate-chunk
    cookies 38
  caramel-filled chocolates 189
  chocolate coconut mint thins
    191
  chocolate-freckled banana
    bread 105
  chocolate honeycomb biscuit
    cake 92
  chocolate leaves 95
  chocolate mousse with
    cappuccino cream 142
  chocolate peanut butter cups
    186
  chocolate puddle puddings 141
  hot chocolate fudge sauce 247
  Jaffa orange cakes 33
  mini marshmallow teacakes 25
  mint chocolate semifreddo 164
  nutty, buttery crisp rice squares
    91
  one-bowl chocolate cake with
    yoghurt ganache 94
  roasted cherry and white
    chocolate brownies 99

tempered chocolate 188
triple chocolate caterpillar cake
  86–9
chocolate hazelnut spread 242
  chocolate hazelnut ice cream
    149
  chocolate hazelnut kisses 185
  chocolate hazelnut toaster
    pastries 71
  triple chocolate caterpillar cake
    86–9
chocolate milk 224
  Irish cream fudge 182
chocolate, milk
  brown butter chocolate-chunk
    cookies 38
  caramel tea and biscuit slice 41
  chocolate hazelnut kisses 185
  chocolate leaves 95
  chocolate peanut butter cups
    186
  Irish cream fudge 182
  malted milk chocolate ice
    cream balls 153
  milk chocolate and honey
    nougat bars 194–6
  milk chocolate hazelnut spread
    242
  tempered chocolate 188
  triple chocolate caterpillar cake
    86–9
chocolate, white
  caramel tea and biscuit slice 41
  caramelised white hot
    chocolate 229
  chocolate leaves 95
  Irish cream fudge 182
  lemon and white chocolate
    éclairs 65
  modelling chocolate 90
  roasted cherry and white
    chocolate brownies 99
cocoa powder 10
  blackberry and hazelnut
    meringue sandwiches 48
  chocolate hazelnut spread 242
  chocolate honeycomb biscuit
    cake 92
  hot chocolate 226
  hot chocolate fudge sauce 247
  one-bowl chocolate cake with

yoghurt ganache 94
real bourbon biscuits 36
roasted cherry and white
  chocolate brownies 98–9
triple chocolate caterpillar cake
  86–9
coconut cream
  sticky date puddings with
    coconut caramel 130
coconut, desiccated
  coconut and raspberry
    Battenberg 100–3
  mini carrot cakes with coconut
    and lime 78
coconut flakes
  coconut brown rice pudding
    124
coconut milk
  coconut and raspberry
    Battenberg 100–3
  coconut brown rice pudding
    124
coffee
  chocolate milk 224
  chocolate mousse with
    cappuccino cream 142
  coffee and walnut choux buns
    65
  frozen maple cappuccino 222
cream cheese
  mini carrot cakes 78
cream, double
  banoffee pecan éclairs 64–5
  blackberry and hazelnut
    meringue sandwiches 48
  British summer mess 116–7
  butterscotch devil's delight 114
  caramelised rice pudding pots
    126
  cheat's crème caramel 121
  chocolate mousse with
    cappuccino cream 142
  coffee and walnut choux buns
    65
  fig and hazelnut bread and
    butter pudding 129
  gooseberry fool 132
  hot chocolate fudge sauce 247
  Irish cream fudge 182
  lemon and white chocolate
    éclairs 65

mini milk lollies 173
mint chocolate semifreddo 164
pear and pecan treacle tart 138
pecan caramel apples/pears 56
rosemary sea salt caramels 192
spiced strawberry layer cake 83
triple chocolate caterpillar cake
  86–9
upside-down lemon meringue
  pie 119
vanilla custard 148
whipped cream 248
cream, single
  caramelised white hot
    chocolate 229
  chocolate milk 224
cream, whipping
  malted milk chocolate ice
    cream balls 153
  sgroppino 220
  custard vanilla 148

dates
  malt whisky loaf 68
  sticky date puddings 130
digestive biscuits
  chocolate honeycomb biscuit
    cake 92
  wholemeal spelt digestives 21
dulce de leche, see milk
  caramel

elderflowers
  gooseberry fool 132

figs, dried
  almond, honey and cinnamon
    fig rolls 28
  fig and rye rock buns 53
figs, fresh
  fig and hazelnut bread and
    butter pudding 129
  flower ice cubes 212

gingerbread 42
  gingerbread crumb ice cream
    163
gooseberries
  gooseberry fool 132
  gooseberry mess 117

grapefruit
   grapefruit curd 244
grapefruit, pink
   ginger and grapefruit
      lemonade 210
   pink grapefruit, ginger and
      poppy-seed cupcakes 76

hazelnuts
   blackberry and hazelnut
      meringue sandwiches 48
   chocolate hazelnut kisses
      184–5
   chocolate hazelnut spread 242
   chocolate hazelnut toaster
      pastries 71
   fig and hazelnut bread and
      butter pudding 129
   nut butter 238
herb ice cubes 212
honeycomb 197
   chocolate honeycomb biscuit
      cake 92

ice cream 149–51
   chocolate-coated ice cream
      bars 154
   cinnamon breadcrumb ice
      cream 162–3
   gingerbread crumb ice cream
      163
   mix-ins 176
   peanut butter and jam Arctic
      roll 157
Irish cream fudge 182

jam
   apricot, jam and amaretto tart
      134–5
   caramelised rice pudding pots
      126
   coconut and raspberry
      Battenberg 100–3
   jam-packed doughnuts 61–3
   peanut butter and jam Arctic
      roll 157
   peanut butter and jammie
      dodgers 18
   spiced strawberry layer cake 83
   strawberry ripple ice cream 150
   wholemeal toaster pastries 71

kiwi and mint ice lollies 172

lemon curd 244
   lemon and white chocolate
      éclairs 65
   lemon ice cream 151
   upside-down lemon meringue
      pie 119
lemons
   blackberry and apple pastilles
      198
   blackcurrant, blueberry and
      mint cordial 213
   blueberry, almond and plum
      crumble 110
   British summer mess 116–7
   caramel tea and biscuit slice 41
   coconut and raspberry
      Battenberg 100–3
   lemon and thyme creams 34
   lemon curd 244
   lemon sorbet 170
   nectarine upside-down cake 81
   orange blossom Turkish
      delight 200
   rhubarb jelly and ice cream
      with cardamom crunch 113
   rosemary lemonade 210
   sgroppino 220
limes
   lime curd 244
   mini carrot cakes with coconut
      and lime 78
   pineapple and ginger ice lollies
      172
   pistachio and lime loaf 84
liquorice 202

malt extract 11
   malt whisky loaf 68
   malted milk chocolate ice
      cream balls 153
mango and chilli ice lollies 172
maple syrup
   chocolate milk 224
   coffee and walnut choux buns
      65
   frozen maple cappuccino 222
   rhubarb jelly and ice cream
      with cardamom crunch 113

whipped cream 248
marshmallows
   caramelised white hot
      chocolate 229
   hot chocolate 226
   nutty, buttery crisp rice squares
      91
   peppermint marshmallows
      204
meringues
   blackberry and hazelnut
      meringue sandwiches 48
   British summer mess 116–7
   foolish mess 132
   peach melba baked Alaska
      158–9
   upside-down lemon meringue
      pie 119
milk caramel 246
   banoffee pecan éclairs 64–5
   caramel-filled chocolates 189
   caramel ice cream 151
   caramel tea and biscuit slice 41
milkshakes 176

nectarines
   nectarine upside-down cake 81
nougat 194

oranges
   almond, honey and cinnamon
      fig rolls 28
   apricot, peanut and sesame
      flapjacks 54
   British summer mess 116–7
   fig and hazelnut bread and
      butter pudding 129
   fig and rye rock buns 53
   Jaffa orange cakes 33
   mini carrot cakes 78
   orange and honey iced buns
      60
   orange blossom Turkish
      delight 200
   orange, cardamom and poppy-
      seed shortbread 30
   orange curd 244
   rhubarb jelly and ice cream
      with cardamom crunch 113
   spiced gingerbread 42
   spiced strawberry, orange and

almond layer cake 83
peaches
    peach and mint iced tea 219
    peach melba baked Alaska
        158–9
    raspberry and peach jam 239
peanut butter 238
    apricot, peanut and sesame
        flapjacks 54
    chocolate peanut butter cups
        186
    chocolate peanut butter sauce
        247
    mini peanut butter teacakes 25
    nutty, buttery crisp rice squares
        91
    peanut butter and jam Arctic
        roll 157
    peanut butter and jammie
        dodgers 18
pears
    pear and pecan treacle tart 138
    pecan caramel pears 56
pecans
    banoffee pecan éclairs 64–5
    chocolate honeycomb biscuit
        cake 92
    pear and pecan treacle tart 138
    pecan caramel apples/pears 56
Pimm's: British summer mess
    117
pineapple and ginger ice lollies
    172
pistachio nuts
    coconut brown rice pudding
        124
    mini carrot cakes 78
    pistachio and lime loaf 84
plums
    blueberry, almond and plum
        crumble 110
    strawberry, plum and vanilla
        jam 239
polenta
    nectarine upside-down cake
        81
pomegranates
    coconut brown rice pudding
        124
popcorn 59
poppy seeds

orange, cardamom and poppy-
    seed shortbread 30
pink grapefruit, ginger and
    poppy-seed cupcakes 76
prosecco
    Aperol spritz 216
    sgroppino 220
prunes: malt whisky loaf 68

raisins
    malt whisky loaf 68
    oat and buttermilk scones 50
raspberries
    coconut and raspberry
        Battenberg 100–3
    peach melba baked Alaska
        158–9
    raspberry and peach jam 239
    upside-down lemon meringue
        pie 119
rhubarb
    rhubarb jelly 113
    rhubarb mess 117
rice
    caramelised rice pudding pots
        126
    coconut brown rice pudding
        124
rice cereal
    nutty, buttery crisp rice squares
        91
rolled oats
    apricot, peanut and sesame
        flapjacks 54
    blueberry, almond and plum
        crumble 110
    mini marshmallow teacakes
        24–5
    oat and buttermilk scones 50
    oaty dunkers 22
    rhubarb jelly and ice cream
        with cardamom crunch 113
    wholemeal spelt digestives 21

sherbet 202
strawberries
    British summer mess 116–7
    spiced strawberry layer cake 83
    strawberry and basil ice lollies
        172
    strawberry, plum and vanilla

jam 239
sultanas
    coconut brown rice pudding
        124
    malt whisky loaf 68
    oat and buttermilk scones 50
sundaes 176

tea
    caramel tea and biscuit slice 41
    malt whisky loaf 68
    oat and buttermilk scones 50
    peach and mint iced tea 219
treacle
    malt whisky loaf 68

vanilla extract 249
vodka
    sgroppino 220
    vanilla extract 249

walnuts
    coffee and walnut choux buns
        65
wheatgerm
    mini marshmallow teacakes
        24–5
    oaty dunkers 22
    wholemeal spelt digestives 21
whisky
    butterscotch devil's delight 114
    chocolate milk 224
    malt whisky loaf 68

yoghurt, Greek
    chocolate-freckled banana
        bread 105
    gooseberry fool 132
    soft-serve ice cream 168
    spiced strawberry layer cake 83
    upside-down lemon meringue
        pie 119
yoghurt, natural
    oat and buttermilk scones 50
    one-bowl chocolate cake with
        yoghurt ganache 94

THANK YOU

First and foremost to my readers – to anyone who has bought this book, or who reads *The Little Loaf* blog, or both. It's an honour to be invited into your kitchens. If you didn't exist, neither would this book, so thank you from the bottom of my heart.

I am especially grateful to my army of recipe testers, from best friends and family in London to blog readers I've never met on the other side of the world. Lauren Bradley, Olivia Campbell, Lucy Charles, Phoebe Cheshire, Jenny Chrimes, Joyce Dooley, Jessica Frawley, Alice Harries, Rosie Hooper, Camilla Lawson, Rachel Levett, Celia Lister, Emma Pollock, Beth Spicer, Victoria Talbot, Fiona Wallace, Max Webster and Susannah Webster – you are all awesome.

To Hellie Ogden, my agent, for being generally fabulous and for guiding me through the complicated process of publishing a cookbook.

To Amanda Harris for believing in this project and to Kate Wanwimolruk, my editor, for shaping it into this thing that I'm so incredibly proud of. Big thank yous also to Helen and Arielle, Mark, Alice, Tamsin and the rest of the team at Orion. And to Laura Nickoll for your amazing eagle eyes.

To Helen Cathcart, I have no words. Your photographs are breathtaking; I adore them. Thank you to River and Kevin too for your stellar assistance (both photographing and eating).

To Hen Clancy and your magical Mary Poppins-style toolbox. Thank you so much for all your hard work (and those amazing scrambled eggs). And to lovely Linda Berlin, the Father Christmas of prop shopping.

To my wonderful grandparents, you may no longer be with us, but you live on in so many fond memories. And Great Aunt Pam who invented – so to speak – 'The Little Loaf'.

Mum, Dad, Max – hooray for greedy Webster genes! A lifetime of love, encouragement and more meals cooked and shared than I can count can't be summarised in a few sentences. Suffice to say I love you all infinitely and I wouldn't be where I am today without you.

Finally, to Luke, you make life sweeter than any homemade treat. Thank you for your unwavering support throughout this process, for having more confidence in me than I do, for tasting anything and everything with such endless enthusiasm and for making me smile through all the difficult bits. Everyone needs a Luke in their life. I love you.

First published in Great Britain in 2015
by Orion Publishing Group Ltd
Carmelite House, 50 Victoria Embankment
London EC4Y ODZ
An Hachette UK Company

1 3 5 7 9 10 8 6 4 2

Text © Kate Doran 2015
Design and layout © Orion Publishing Group Ltd 2015

ISBN: 978 1 4091 5579 9

Photography © Helen Cathcart
Designer: Arielle Gamble
Props stylist: Linda Berlin
Home economist assistant: Henrietta Clancy
Copy editor: Laura Nickoll
Project editor: Kate Wanwimolruk

Printed and bound in China

The Orion Publishing Group's policy is to use papers that are natural,
renewable and recyclable products and made from wood grown in
sustainable forests. The logging and manufacturing processes are expected
to conform to the environmental regulations of the country of origin.

www.orionbooks.co.uk